T0195087

WHAT WILL GET US THROUGH?

*Messages of Hope,
Encouragement, and Peace*

Reverend Patricia A. Turner-Brown

authorHOUSE®

AuthorHouse™
1663 Liberty Drive
Bloomington, IN 47403
www.authorhouse.com
Phone: 833-262-8899

Published by AuthorHouse 06/14/2022

ISBN: 978-1-6655-4777-2 (sc)
ISBN: 978-1-6655-4778-9 (hc)
ISBN: 978-1-6655-4784-0 (e)

Library of Congress Control Number: 2021925658

Print information available on the last page.

Photo Credit: Miles Photography

Interior Image Credit: Kyle Perrilloux

This book is printed on acid-free paper.

About the Author

Reverend Dr. Patricia A. Turner-Brown attended the Detroit Public Schools, graduating from the prestigious Cass Technical High School as an instrumental music major. Following her graduation from high school, she matriculated at Western Michigan University in Kalamazoo, MI, receiving the Bachelor of Music in Music Education. She furthered her education by receiving the Master of Music Education from Wayne State University. "Rev. Pat" taught instrumental and vocal music in the school districts of Detroit (MI), Highland Park (MI), Atlanta (GA), and New Orleans (LA). Her students benefited from her kind spirit and gentle prod for their success as students and human beings.

Her educational pursuits continued as she earned the Master of Divinity degree from Turner Theological Seminary/Interdenominational Theological Center in Atlanta, Ga., and the Doctor of Ministry degree from the Ecumenical Theological Seminary in Detroit, MI. "Rev Pat" has served on the ministerial staffs of Allen Temple AME Church (Atlanta),

Christ United Methodist Church (Detroit), Brooks United Methodist Church (New Orleans), and Bethel AME Church (Baton Rouge), and as the Youth Pastor of her home church Ebenezer AME Detroit. She has also pastored churches in both the United Methodist Church (Trinity UMC-New Orleans) and the African Methodist Episcopal Church (McMichael AME, Amite, Louisiana).

"Rev. Pat" is married to the Reverend Dr. Lance E. Brown, a retired minister of the United Methodist Church. They are the parents of three adult children, six grandchildren, and one great-grandson.

As a student at the ITC, "Rev. Pat" was inducted into the International Honor Society of Theta Phi. She is an active member of Alpha Kappa Alpha Sorority, Inc., and Sigma Alpha Iota International Music Fraternity.

The scripture which guides Rev. Pat on her faith journey is Proverbs 3:5-6 (NIV) "Trust in the Lord with all your heart and lean not on your own understanding. In all your ways acknowledge him, and he will make your path straight. Her faith is further undergirded by her personal motto, "If you make the effort, God will make the way!"

With Covid 19, it is imperative that we not lose hope.
"What Will Get Us Through?"
will direct readers to where hope, encouragement,
and peace can be found.

Foreword

It is with honor and humility that I pen this Foreword for the Reverend Dr. Patricia A. Turner Brown, my sister. Born and raised in the city of Detroit, MI, she is one of four children. Her parents had a strong belief and conviction that all their children would be musicians. Diverse in her musical abilities, she played violin, viola, piano, French horn, and tuba, and sung in her school choirs.

"Rev. Pat" attended Ebenezer African Methodist Episcopal Church (Detroit), with her parents and siblings. As an active member of the Youth Department, she served on the usher board, sang in the Youth Choir, and assisted in the Youth Church. Loving the outdoors, she also attended the AME Church 4th Episcopal District Summer Camp Programs at Camp Baber in Cassopolis, MI. Additional church activities included trips with the Youth Department to various states during the summer. As a young adult, she became very active in the Lay Organization of the AME Church, attending conferences, and learning more about God, the structure of the AME Church, and most importantly her personal journey with God

Often, we may choose to follow the most popular route of doing what others think we should do. We may choose not to heed to the tugging in our hearts and minds. However, there comes a time in our lives where we must be obedient to the beckoning of God. In following His footsteps, one can never go wrong. It is rare to witness someone submit to a true calling in their life.

In the world of orchestras and bands, one loves to have the honor of being "first chair" in a section. I sat in the "first chair" position as I witnessed "Rev. Pat" preach her trial sermon at Ebenezer AME Church. I sat in "first chair, as I watched her receive her Masters of Divinity Degree from Interdenominational Theological Center. I sat in "first chair" as I watched her receive her Doctor of Ministry from Ecumenical Theological Seminary. I salute her from the honored position of seeing her in "First Chair" for her book of heartfelt sermons, *"What Will Get Us Through"* which will encourage us all.

With Much Love Eternally,
Sylvia T. Hollifield, Ph.D.

Acknowledgements

I first acknowledge and thank God, who through God's Son Jesus the Christ, and empowered by the Holy Spirit, called me to be a messenger of God's Word. I did not immediately respond to that call, but I thank you Lord for not giving up on me.

I acknowledge and thank my parents, the late Talmage Lorenzo and Rosa Brezzell Turner for instilling in my heart and spirit a love for family, and love for God and THE CHURCH. It was through my upbringing in Ebenezer African Methodist Episcopal Church in Detroit, Michigan, and the spiritual guidance of its wonderful pastors that my love of church and the Word of God grew and that it continues to grow. I also thank my parents for implanting in me (as well as my siblings) the love of music.

I thank my husband, the Reverend Dr. Lance E. Brown, a retired United Methodist minister, who sees my sermons as being worthy of being compiled into a book to share with others. Thank you for your encouragement, and for being my rock and "cheering section" during this entire process. Throughout my pastoral ministry, he has been actively supportive and has always "had my back!" Thank you "Babe!"

I thank the Reverend Dr. Carolyn Ann Knight, former Assistant Professor of Homiletics at the Interdenominational Theological Center in Atlanta, Georgia (my alma mater) who took the time to read and critique my messages to make sure they are exegetical, hermeneutically and homiletically sound, and that they have practical application.

I thank my sister, Dr. Sylvia Turner-Hollifield for consenting to write the Forward. She has known me from day one and throughout my life's journey. She has the insight that only a sister could have.

I acknowledge my father in the ministry, the late Bishop Robert Thomas, Jr., whose sage words of advice have remained with me throughout my ministry- "Love the people, preach the gospel simple and free, and be led by the Holy Spirit."

Although I no longer serve as their pastor, I must also acknowledge the members of McMichael African Methodist Episcopal Church in Amite, Louisiana, to whom I was able to minister to in word and deed.

Introduction

"WHAT WILL GET US THROUGH?"

Except for "**Don't Let The Devil Fool Ya!**" preached on March 1, 2020, before the church doors were closed due to the pandemic, the 26 messages included in this compilation of messages were all preached to the members of McMichael African Methodist Episcopal Church in Amite Louisiana via the phone conference call platform.

I believe two pertinent questions that were foremost in our minds regarding the COVID-19 pandemic were "when will this virus end? After about two months and no immediate end in sight, the second question became "what's going to get us through this pandemic?"

In addition to the trying time of the pandemic, the nation, especially the African-American community was in an upheaval caused by the unjustified and malicious deaths of George Floyd, Breonna Taylor, Jacob Flakes, Ahmaud Ambery, and others. This led to many protests and riots.

And then, there was a person in the White House who, despite the advice from the medical and scientific community denied the seriousness of the virus. The political climate of the country was also brewing with the upcoming presidential election as "45" continued to host unmasked "super-spreader" political rallies. He offered no significant leadership to help curb the virus. That is why at every opportunity, the congregation was encouraged to put into practice the **"Stewardship of Citizenship"** by exercising their right to vote to change the occupant of 1600 Pennsylvania Ave.

This unprecedented virus changed our entire way of living. Businesses, stores, schools, and houses of worship were closed. Shelter in place, wash your hands frequently, use hand sanitizer, wear a mask, social distance became the mandated directives of the day. Many jobs were lost due to business shut-downs, which created economic hardships for many families. This stress caused a rise in emotional and mental challenges and an increase in domestic violence.

We know that many persons contracted the virus and lost their lives. Emotional family stress was created because family members were not able to visit ill family members in the hospital, and even harder, to be present with a loved one as they transitioned from their earthly life to eternal life. But we praise God for the many more who overcame Covid-19.

It was my prayer that as I prepared these messages "for such a time as this," I would be guided by the Holy Spirit to deliver a Word that would offer peace (**Perfect *Peace***), encouragement (**Yes There Is!**), salvation (**God's Gift of Repentance**), God's protection (**Refuge at the Lord's Table**), and a desire within the hearer to have a closer relationship with God (**Sheltered in Place**).

Despite the pandemic, the multiple hardships, challenges, and changes it has caused in our lives, the systemic racism that remains prevalent in our society, and the political climate, that through it all, we would know in our heart, our mind, and our spirit, what could get us through these hard times. As you read, visualize, and hear these messages in your heart, mind, and spirit, it is my prayer that you will be able to answer the question **"WHAT WILL GET US THROUGH?"**

Contents

PRAYER-RELATIONSHIPS

ASSURANCE-TRUST

SPECIAL DAYS

PRAYER-RELATIONSHIPS

WHY PRAY?

Philippians 4: 4-9

While in line at Wal-Mart, I overheard a conversation between the two gentlemen who were ahead of me. The conversation centered around the pandemic, which morphed into the killing of George Floyd and the protest and riots that have followed and are ongoing. "Man, this is the worst thing I've ever seen. All these folks getting sick and dying, the way they are killing our people, and on top of all of that an impending hurricane. He went on and on. He was venting. The other man just listened. He then calmly responded with "Hey man, God will get us through all of this. We just have to keep praying." The first man looked shocked and even perturbed. He asked the question "Why pray? What good is that going to do?" Before the question could be answered, it was his turn to pay for his items, then he departed. I caught the other gentleman's eye and nodded, Amen!

The question of "why pray?" stuck with me, and I'm going to attempt to answer that question. The first reason is that God wants to have a deep and intimate relationship with us. Just like regular communication nurtures any relationship we have, be it a marital relationship, relationships with your children, or a relationship with your "boo," communication is certainly necessary for a strong relationship with God. We need to communicate with God daily. God wants us to speak to Him in prayer long enough for us to sense and hear what God has to say. Yes, we pray on the fly, because the Word of God tells us to (1st Thessalonians 5:17 KJV) *"pray without ceasing."* However, we should pray so we can have a dialogue with God. We talk to God, and God talks to us. It is a dialogue, not a monologue. We have to take the time to listen.

It's been scientifically proven that when we pray and spend time with God, we are healthier, happier, and more secure in life. We become more concerned about others, which leads us to lifting them in prayer. Know that prayer changes things, changes people, and changes you and me.

And then we should pray because this is the way we express our needs and desires to God. Yes, God knows what we have need of, even more than we know ourselves. But God wants to hear it from our lips, and our heart. Prayer is the means of obtaining solutions in a number of situations. God has promised that when we ask for things that are in the will of God, God will give us what we ask for. Prayer should not be seen as our means of getting God to do our will on earth, but rather as a means of getting God's will done on earth.

A lack of prayer shows a lack of faith and a lack of trust in God's Word. We pray to demonstrate our faith in God, that God will do as God has promised in God's Word and bless our lives abundantly more than we could ever ask or hope for. Because prayer is our means of "plugging" into God's power, it is our means of defeating satan and his adversaries that we are powerless to overcome by ourselves. We have the promise of God that (James 5:16 KJV) *"The effectual fervent prayer of a righteous man availeth much."*

As we continue in this valley of COVID-19, it is imperative my brothers and sisters, that we *"pray without ceasing."* (1st Thessalonians 5:17 KJV) We must pray that in the name of Jesus, this virus will subside, that the illnesses and deaths attributed to this disease will lessen and cease, and that we will come out of the valley renewed, revived, rejuvenated, and recommitted to have a closer walk with God.

And then, we must pray for what is going on in this country now. Racism, perpetuated by "45," has again raised its ugly head and has come to the forefront of our society. White supremist have "come out of the closet" and are making their presence known. Our people continue to be shot and killed by rouge police officers and white vigilantes. The protest and riots are our people standing up and saying enough is enough! I don't agree with the violence and destruction of property, because it takes the focus off of the main reason for the protest. However, it does call attention to the systemic problem of racial injustice in this country.

When you rise in the morning, acknowledge who God is, and then thank God for the night's rest. Ask God to order your steps for the day. Pray for God's protection throughout the day. Pray for your family, pray for your church. Pray for those who are on the frontline, who risk their lives day after day for others. I saw a FB post that said, "Every night forgive those who hurt you, pray for those who need it, and thank God for everything you have."

In Ephesians 6:18 NIV, Paul wrote *"And pray in the Spirit on all occasions with all kinds of prayers and request."* How can we pray on all occasions? One way is to make quick brief prayers your habitual response to every situation you encounter throughout the day. Pray for something as basic as thanking God for that good parking space, or praying for that homeless person you are unable to help in a tangible way. Pray for the safety of the firefighters on the firetruck that you had to pulled over for. We don't have to isolate ourselves from other people and our daily routine in order to pray constantly, to keep that line of communication with God open.

Our hope is that we have the assurance of knowing that when we can call on the Lord, in and out of season, that God hears and answers our prayers. As Paul told those in Philippi, (Philippians 4:6-7 KJV) *⁶"Be careful for nothing, but in everything by prayer and supplication with thanksgiving, let your request be made known unto God. ⁷And the peace of God, which transcends all understanding, will guard your hearts and your minds in Jesus Christ"*

Let Us Pray: Lord God, I thank you for hearing and answering my prayers. In Jesus name I pray, Amen.

THE "OTHER" LORD'S PRAYER

John 16: 33; John 17

Today marks the end of my second full year plus eight months, as the pastor of McMichael AME Church. I became your pastor at the 8th Episcopal District March 2018 Mid-Year Convocation. As we prepare for the 2020 Louisiana Annual Conference October 29-30, technically, this is my last Sunday because each appointment is just for one year.

Looking at the journey of 2019-2020, it has been a year marked by ecstatic joys and discouraging lows. It has been marked by times of gladness and times of sadness. It has been marked by times of great togetherness and fellowship, and times of disunity and misunderstanding. But by God's grace, through it all, we as a congregation are still here. Despite not being able to gather together to worship face to face because of the coronavirus which has ravaged, and continues to ravage the world, this country, our state, our community, and families, we are still here as the McMichael AME Church family, praising God, lifting our voices in thanksgiving, and standing on the promise that God will see us through. I believe from the bottom of my heart, that "When WE make the effort, God will make the way!!" Amen!

For a few moments, I would like to share from the subject, **"The "Other" Lord's Prayer"** From the scripture that will be read, we will learn that Jesus is praying to his heavenly Father. Jesus knows he is about to depart this earthly realm, and he understands why he came and took on the form of humanity. Jesus had spent three years with his disciples, not two years and eight months, but three years, teaching them through precept and example how to live life in and for Christ. He spent three years training, preparing them as disciples, so that they could into the highways

4

and byways to teach others and bring them to the saving grace of Jesus the Christ. Now, his time had come to depart from them.

Following the Passover Feast, which was the night Jesus was betrayed by Judas, Jesus spent time talking with his disciples, giving them final instruction, preparing them for his death and resurrection, and life after his departure. Chapters 13-16 give an account of this after-dinner conversation. Please take the time to read those chapters. These chapters take us to the heart of what Jesus wanted for his disciples. The last verse of chapter 16 reads (John 16:33 NIV) *"I have told you these things, so that in me you may have peace. In this world, you will have trouble. But take heart. I have overcome the world."* With these words, he is telling his disciples not to be afraid, to take courage, to be strong. He was letting them know that despite the foreseeable struggles they would face, they would never be alone.

As Jesus finished his conversation with his disciples, he wanted to be alone, to have some quiet time with his heavenly Father. This is a lesson for all of us. Throughout his ministry, regardless of how hectic or chaotic things got, Jesus always took the time to get away from the crowd for personal prayer, meditation, and time with his heavenly Father. Can we as believers afford to do any less? We too, my brothers and sisters must take the time to read, study, and meditate on the Word of God, and to spend time with God in prayer. Amen!

Jesus is now alone in the Garden of Gethsemane, which is on the Mount of Olives. He asked James, John, and Peter, his inner circle to remain with him for a while. It had been a long day, and unfortunately, tired and probably exhausted, the three disciples fell asleep. Jesus is now alone in prayer with his heavenly Father, knowing that following his impending agonizing ordeal, he will soon be in the presence of God. This prayer, which is the "other" Lord's Prayer, is divided into three sections. Jesus first prayed for himself, then he prayed for his disciples, and finally for future believers. So that we can experience its full impact, I will read each section.

First of all, Jesus prayed for Himself. (John 17:1-5 NIV) [1] *After Jesus said this, he looked toward heaven and prayed: "Father, the hour has come. Glorify your Son, that your Son may glorify you.* [2] *For you granted him authority over all people that he might give eternal life to all those you have given him.* ³ *Now this is eternal life: that they know you, the only true God, and Jesus Christ, whom you have sent.* ⁴ *I have brought you glory on earth by finishing the work you gave me to do.* ⁵ *And now, Father, glorify me in your presence with the glory I had with you before the world began.*

When Jesus prayed for God to "glorify His Son," was Jesus being selfish or self-centered? No indeed! Know, my brothers and sisters, that it is always appropriate to ask God for strength, determination, perseverance, and yes, even glory, if the request seeks to bring ultimate glory to God. You must pray for yourself to receive wisdom and guidance, and for God's will to be done in your life.

It is the same thing with our physical bodies. You cannot take care of others if you don't take care of yourself. This is especially true when you are in a position of leadership, be it clergy or lay. It is imperative, of utmost importance that we keep ourselves prayed up, because satan is always busy, on his job 24/7. If satan can get to the head, that is the leadership, then he can get to the whole body. When I pray for myself, I always ask God to give me the wisdom, strength, courage, patience, and love to lead God's people. Did I always get it right? No, I did not! There have been mistakes made along the way. Some members may have been offended by something I might have said or done or did not say or do. As we end this 2019-2020 conference year and embark on 2020-2021, I ask that you forgive me. And I ask that as you pray for yourselves, that you also pray for your pastor.

Next, Jesus prayed for His disciples. (John 17: 6, 9-10, 11b, 15-17 NIV) ⁶ *"I have revealed you to those whom you gave me out of the world. They were yours; you gave them to me and they have obeyed your word…⁹ I pray for them. I am not praying for the world, but for those you have given me, for they are yours.* ¹⁰ *All I have is yours, and all you have is mine. And glory has come to me through them…¹¹ᵇ Holy Father, protect them by the power of your name, the name you gave me, so that they may be one as we are one…¹⁵ My prayer is not that you take them out of the world but that you protect them from the evil one.* ¹⁶ *They are not of the world, even as I am not of it.* ¹⁷ *Sanctify them by the truth; your word is truth.*

Jesus was concerned for his disciples because he knew what they would have to face. Jesus begins by telling God that I revealed to those you gave me who you are, which they understood and accepted. The disciples believed the things taught to them concerning God. In other words, Jesus taught them by precept and example. Not only did they come to know God through the words Jesus taught them, but also by his actions. They not only knew of God, but they also knew God for themselves.

Jesus makes it clear that he is praying for the disciples and not the world. Jesus prays that as he leaves them to carry on in his name, that God will protect them by the power of God's name. Why? So that they may be one. Jesus is praying that the disciples will be united in harmony and love, just as the Father, Son, and Holy Spirit are one. This is the strongest of all unities. McMichael! We must be united as a church family, as one. Yes, we know there is a division in our church family. But like when Paul and Barnabas went their separate ways, the result was the Word of God continued to be spread. We can be one in body and spirit and at the same time have the Word of God being shared. It is a matter of it being done decently and in order.

Again, Jesus knows what the disciples must face. He knows the world will hate them because the world hated him. Jesus prays that the disciples will not be taken out of the world, but that God will protect them from the evil one, that they will be able to stand firm and strong against the adversary and "his crew."

The Savior then prays for them to be sanctified. A true believer becomes set apart for sacred use and is cleansed and made holy through believing and obeying the Word of God. I spoke about sanctification and holiness last Sunday. Again, holiness is growing into the likeness of God and being consecrated, set aside for God's use. True believers know that the daily application of the Word of God has a purifying effect on our hearts, minds, and spirits. This helps us to grow in the likeness of God and Jesus Christ. A true believer has accepted forgiveness through Jesus Christ's sacrificial death.

My prayer for you McMichael, is that you will be unified in the love and strength of God, so that when satan rears his ugly head, and he will, you will be able to stand strong, in the might of God's word, individually and collectively, as a church family, as biological family members, and strongly, firmly, and boldly declare... "Satan, get thee behind!" I pray that you take your rightful place as a sanctified body of believers, set apart from the world to do the will of God.

I also pray that as you pray for yourselves, both individually and as

7

a body of believers, that you will be strengthened, that you will remain steadfast, that you will remain in the will of God, and that you will be the disciples of Christ and witnesses to the love and saving grace of God the Father Almighty. I pray for you to be abundantly blessed so that you may be a blessing to others, that you serve God by serving and ministering to others, especially those in need. My prayer is that the world, your community, your families will see Christ in and through you.

Finally, Jesus prayed for future believers. (John 17:20-26 NIV) [20] *"My prayer is not for them alone. I pray also for those who will believe in me through their message, [21] that all of them may be one, Father, just as you are in me and I am in you. May they also be in us so that the world may believe that you have sent me. [22] I have given them the glory that you gave me, that they may be one as we are one: [23] I in them and you in me—so that they may be brought to complete unity. Then the world will know that you sent me and have loved them even as you have loved me. [24] "Father, I want those you have given me to be with me where I am, and to see my glory, the glory you have given me because you loved me before the creation of the world. [25] "Righteous Father, though the world does not know you, I know you, and they know that you have sent me. [26] I have made you known to them, and will continue to make you known in order that the love you have for me may be in them and that I myself may be in them."*

Jesus prayed for all who would follow Him, including you and me. Jesus' desire for His disciples, present, and future was that they would become one. As Paul said, (Galatians 3:28 NIV) *"…neither Greek nor Jew, slave nor free, male nor female, for you are all one in Jesus Christ."* We would all be a complete unified body of believers, who will be a powerful witness to the reality of God's love.

As we look at our Christian walk, individually and collectively, are the prayers of Jesus being answered, or according to our actions, is Jesus' prayer in vain? Are you helping to unify the Body of Christ and McMichael? Are you praying for others, telling others about God's saving grace, building others up through encouragement, working together in humility (no big I's and little U's)? Or are you spreading rumors and gossip, "shoo-shooing," doing, and saying things that cause disunity and division in the church? Are you giving of your time, talent, and treasure for the cause of Christ, the building up of the kingdom of God, and of McMichael? Or, are you being sidetracked from God's call on your life by arguing over divisive matters, things that can tear us apart as a church body? Most of all, are you exalting the name of Jesus Christ? My prayer is that you, we, will be unified as a church body, so that we can go forth in Jesus' name, bringing others into the saving grace of our Lord and Savior.

My beloved brothers and sisters of McMichael, as we begin a new conference year, know that every day I pray for myself, that as your pastor, God will grant me the wisdom, knowledge, courage, and love to lead and guide you in this trying time of COVID-19, this phase of your spiritual journey, and beyond. And I pray every day for you as a congregation and as individuals, that you will be a body of believers, unified in the Word and love of God. I pray that God will use you to bring others to Christ for the upbuilding of His kingdom here on earth and for the continued life of this church. Again, as we begin a new conference year, my prayer is that when the church doors do re-open, we will be an inviting, loving, encouraging church, inviting family members, friends, neighbors, embracing all who enter, encouraging them to receive Christ as Lord and Savior, the one who forgives and pardons our sins.

I am trusting and believing what Paul wrote to the Philippian Church, (Philippians 1:6 NIV) *"...that he who began a good work in you will carry it on to the day of completion until the day of Jesus Christ."* Everyone, and I do mean everyone has a vital role to play in the life of this church. No one, and again, I do mean no one, can afford to sit back and let eight to ten people do all the work. Embrace and nurture our young people. They are both our present and our future. Know that they copy and imitate what they see us doing. Are we setting a good example?

My prayer for you McMichael is that in the name of Jesus the Christ, you continue to grow in spirit and love. Remember, that "when WE make the effort, God will make the way." It is up to all of us. And just as I pray for you, I ask that you pray for me, that God gives me what I need to lead and guide you, the McMichael church family on your spiritual journey.

Let us pray: Lord God, just as you prayed for yourself, your disciples, and future believers, let us do likewise. Let us pray for ourselves, one another, and for those who will come to know you. In the name of Your Son, Jesus the Christ, Amen.

DON'T LEAVE JESUS BEHIND

Luke 2:41-52 (43-49)

As a parent or guardian, or one responsible for watching a younger sibling, there has probably been at least one occasion when the person you were supposed to be watching got away from you. It could have happened at a department store, at a parade, or in my case at the beach. When my older sister and I were in high school, the two of us and a friend of hers decided we wanted to have a "girl's day" at the beach. My mom said no problem, but we had to take our little brother with us. He was seven years old, and from the tone of Mom's voice, we knew that if he did not go, neither would we.

Long story short, he wandered off. As we searched for him, there was a commotion a little way down the shore. In our moving toward that commotion, we learned that a little black boy around 7 or 8 had drowned. Of course, our hearts sank. All I could think of was my mother was going to kill us for letting something happen to her baby. As we got closer, guess who we see casually and calmly walking toward us. My brother, with a handful of seashells. We grabbed and hugged him, and asked if he was okay. He had no clue as to what was going on. And then my sister let him have it. She walloped him and then fussed at him all the way home about wandering off. The "funny" thing is we threatened him and made him promise not to tell our mom what happened. We still laugh about that 54 years later!

When we look at this passage of scripture, we know that Mary and Joseph, along with their 12-year-old son Jesus traveled to Jerusalem from Nazareth, a three-day journey, to celebrate the Passover. According to Jewish law, every male child was required to go to Jerusalem three times a year to observe the great Jewish festivals. The Passover was celebrated in the spring. Jesus had been making this journey with his parents, probably from the time they returned from the motherland Egypt, so he was familiar with the rituals and celebrations. I am sure he had been looking forward to being old enough to go into the temple to sit and talk with the rabbis. Since he was twelve years old, he might have been preparing for his Bar Mitzvah the following year.

At the age of thirteen, a boy becomes a "son of the commandment," that is, obligated to assume the duties and responsibilities of adult synagogue membership. In modern Judaism, both young men and young ladies celebrate this rite of passage at 13 years old with the Bar Mitzvah and Bat Mitzvah. Following the traditions of many African societies, many of our black churches or civic organizations sponsor Rights of Passage ceremonies for both young ladies and young men.

As they began their journey back to Jerusalem, unbeknownst to Mary and Joseph, Jesus had lingered behind. He had become so engrossed in the teachings and conversations led by these great teachers, that he did not realize his people had departed. Even though he was the Son of God, he assumed the role of the student. His Messiahship had not yet been revealed. As he sat and talked, and respectfully questioned the rabbis, they were astonished, not so much because of his age but because of the depth of his wisdom and knowledge. But that is not surprising. Following his circumcision, and before their departure to the motherland of Egypt, Luke writes (Luke 2:39-40 NIV) [39]*"When Mary and Joseph had done everything required by the law of the Lord, they returned to Galilee to their own town of Nazareth.* [40]*And the child grew and became strong; he was filled with wisdom, and the grace of God was upon him."*

In the meantime, Mary and Joseph realized Jesus was not among their relatives. And at some point, I am sure Jesus realized his people had left him behind. Well, Mary and Joseph returned to Jerusalem. After searching, his parents did find him, in the Temple, with the rabbis. With a tone of great concern, and reprimand, which would be normal for any upset mother, (Luke 2:48 NIV) *"Mary asked him, "Why have you done this to us? Your Father and I have been anxiously searching for you."* The Good News Translation puts it this way. *"His parents were astonished when they saw Him, and his mother said to Him, "Son, why have you done this to us? Your father and I have been terribly worried trying to find you."*

Understand now, Jesus had not hidden from them nor did he defy their authority. After all, they left him. Rather than wandering around looking for them, he remained where he was. He was in the Temple, a public place, safe, with trusted adults, and he was having a good time. Jesus responded to his mother, (Luke 2: 49 NKJV) *⁴⁹"Why did you seek me? Did you not know I must be about my Father's business?"* These are the first recorded words of Jesus. His reply was in no way rude or disrespectful. He was amazed that they did not know where to look for him. This also reveals that at an early age, Jesus had a clear understanding of His identity and His mission.

However, Jesus' relationship to His heavenly father in no way diminished His duty to His earthly parents. He was obedient to the 5th commandment (Exodus 20:12a NIV) to...*honor your father and your mother...* This part of the scripture concludes with (Luke 2:51 NIV) *⁵¹ Then he went down to Nazareth with them and was obedient to them. But his mother treasured all these things in her heart. ⁵² And Jesus grew in wisdom and stature, and in favor with God and men."*

Mary and Joseph unknowingly left Jesus behind. I ask the question, have you left Jesus behind? His parents were so wrapped up in getting back home that they did not realize they had left Jesus behind. Sometimes we can get so wrapped up in what we are doing, that we do leave Jesus behind. In this season of the pandemic, our minds are occupied with "will I contract the virus?" We are busy going to work, to school online, doing essential shopping. Many are busy remaining sheltered in place, cleaning the house, cooking, binge-watching their favorite TV show, surfing the internet. Have you taken the time to spend time with God and Jesus Christ by making reading, meditating, and reflecting on God's Word a priority? Have you taken time to spend time with God through Jesus Christ in prayer? In our busyness, let us not leave Jesus behind.

When Mary and Joseph discovered Jesus had been left behind, they went back to Jerusalem to look for him, but initially were looking in the wrong places. When we realize we have left Jesus behind, where do we look? Jesus' parents found him in the Temple, learning about God. If learning was a priority for Jesus, it should be just as important for us. This is about Church School, Bible Study, and digging into the Word of God. Know something about the writers and who they were writing to. Know something about the culture.

And then learn how you can apply God's Word to your life. It was Kasi Kaye Ilipoulos who said "Knowledge without application is merely knowledge. Applying the knowledge to one's life is wisdom…." The Bible is our source of guidance on how we are to live. Remember, 2ⁿᵈ Tim. 3:16-17 NIV tells us *16 "All Scripture is God-breathed and is useful for teaching, rebuking, correcting and training in righteousness, 17 so that the servant of God may be <u>thoroughly</u> equipped for every good work."*

The word of God leads us to finding Jesus. I ask the question, "Have you left Jesus behind in your life?" If so, I encourage you to find Him as quickly as you can and put things in place, like having that relationship with God through Jesus Christ, and the guidance of the Holy Spirit. This will ensure that you will find Him. My brothers and sisters DON'T LEAVE JESUS BEHIND!

Let us pray: Lord God, please let me not "clutter" my life with so much "stuff", that I leave Your Son out. Cleanse my life so that Jesus is the center of my life. In the matchless name of Jesus Christ I pray, Amen..

ONE IN MANY-MANY IN ONE

1st Corinthians 12:4-11

On the first Sunday, I spoke about the church in Corinth, and the problems they were having being the church. There was division in the church caused by its members creating chaos about the preachers and who followed who. They were not properly following the true purpose and intentions of the Agape Meal or Love Feast nor the Sacrament of Holy Communion. They were trying to be the church God was calling them to be, but they had a lot to overcome.

Most of the members of the Corinthian Church had come out of the Greek culture of Corinth, which meant they had grown up in a place that worshipped pagan gods, where prostitution was legal, and where there was a high tolerance for lax morals standards and freedom of thought. Most members of the church had been born and raised in this culture. Even though they had accepted Christ, their culture was still deeply rooted in them. They brought with them to the church the ideas, thoughts, and philosophies reflective of their culture. That is like us accepting Christ as our Lord and Savior, but those old negative habits and activities are constantly tempting us, trying to pull us back in. In spite of all they had against them, the Corinthian Church still struggled to be a church committed to the cause of Jesus Christ.

Another problem the Corinthian Church was dealing with was the issue of exercising spiritual gifts. These were, and are gifts and abilities given to individuals who have accepted Christ and His message of salvation. The gifts are given to build up the Kingdom of God and are empowered by the Holy Spirit. Notice that I am using the present, right now tense. Spiritual gifts are also given so that every Christian can experience the joy and fulfillment of God working through his or her life.

These include the gifts of preaching, teaching, serving, prophecy, administration, mercy, giving, exhortation, speaking in tongues, and interpreting tongues. Sometime this week, I ask that you read the entire 12th chapter of 1st Corinthians. Also read Romans 12:4-8, Ephesians 4:11-12, and 1st Peter 4:10-11. These passages of scripture help us to understand the meaning, nature, and purpose of spiritual gifts. As written in the Ephesian passage, these gifts are given by God and empowered by the Holy Spirit to (Ephesians 4:12-13 NIV) *12"...equip his people* [those who have accepted Christ as their Lord and Savior] *for the works of service, so that the Body of Christ may be built up, 13until we all of reach unity in faith and in the knowledge of the Son of God, and become mature, attaining the whole measure of the fullness of Christ"* On a personal note, it is on this premise that God revealed to me that this was my purpose in ministry, that is, to equip, to teach the saints for the work of ministry.

Paul is telling us that spiritual gifts are not given for self-glory or to build one's ego, but to build up the Kingdom of God. Instead of unifying the church and strengthening the Corinthian Church, like the issues of the messengers, and the Love Feast and Communion, it was splitting and tearing down the church. Some had become excessively proud of their showier gifts such as preaching, teaching, and speaking in tongues. They used their gifts as badges of spiritual power. And then those with less showy gifts such as visiting the sick and those in prison, or those who took the time to listen to the problems of others, or those who prayed for those in need, were made to feel that they had little to contribute. Once again, Paul had to get them straight.

Now instead of going through a long, drawn-out lecture about how wrong they were, Paul chose to teach them in a way they could understand. He used something they, and we all have and could and can relate to. He used the example of the human body. Like Christ, Paul was good at creating relevant mental pictures. Each part of the human body has a specific role to play. Even with modern science and technology, the human body cannot naturally function and run as smoothly as it should if one of the components, such as the brain, the heart, the lungs, or our senses is missing. Paul wrote (1st Corinthians 12:12 NIV), *"For just as the body is one and has many members, and all members of the body, though many, are one body, so it is with Christ."*

I imagine Paul reminded them that they were a church composed of many different types of people from a variety of backgrounds, with a multitude of gifts, talents, and abilities. However, despite their differences, there was one thing that all believers then and now have in common. That commonality is faith in our Lord and Savior Jesus Christ. It is in this important truth that the church, the Body of Christ finds unity.

To take it a step further, the thread that knits this common faith together in Jesus Christ, and the different gifts and abilities into a unified, yet a diverse body of believers is the indwelling of the Holy Spirit. 1st Corinthians 12:13 NIV) reads *"For we were all baptized by one Spirit so as to form one body—whether Jews or Gentiles, slave or free—* [laity or clergy, trustee or steward or class leader, Sunday School teacher or choir member, educated or uneducated, custodian or cook, haves or have nots, Amite or Independence or Tickfaw or Hammond] *and we were all given the one Spirit to drink. We were all made to drink of the same spirit."* My brothers and sisters, we all have different abilities, and they are all empowered by God, through the Holy Spirit as a means of edifying or building up The Church and our church.

Since we all have different gifts, or even varying degrees of the same gift, we all have different jobs to do. Some are given the responsibility of administration, some the responsibility of teaching, some the responsibility of preaching. Some are called to be prayer intercessors, some called to show mercy, while others are called to give of their material substance.

The bottom line is this. We are all important and essential members of the Body of Christ, and in particular, this body-McMichael AME Church. One of the concepts and terms we hear a lot that has grown out of the Covid-19 pandemic is essential and non-essential workers. Well, my brothers and sisters, I am here to let you know, that as children of God we are all essential workers in the Body of Christ.

I came across some interesting, though broad statements concerning spiritual gifts. Think of how these may apply to you. Prophets are often bold and articulate. Servers are faithful and loyal. Teachers are clear thinkers. Givers are generous and trusting. Administrators are good organizers and managers. Comforters are caring people who are happy to give time to others. Naturally, it would be difficult, actually impossible for one person, such as the pastor to embody all of these gifts. Yet, they are all essential for the Body of Christ to function properly.

So, my brothers and sisters, what's the solution? First of all, use your gift! Offer it to Christ and ask the Lord to help you to develop it to its fullest potential. Not sure of what your gift is? Even before and beyond this pandemic, if what you have been doing in the church seems natural, you enjoy what you are doing, and you are effective, then chances are you are functioning in the realm of your gift. And you know what else? God, in God's infinite wisdom, has a way of matching together our general personalities with our spiritual gifts. Now, unfortunately, some come in and do not exercise the gifts that God has given them. That is like someone with good eyesight coming into the church and keeping their eyes closed, bumping into everything, and not using what God has given them. Let that marinate for a moment. All parts of the body are necessary for The Body to function properly.

Second, do not try to be what you are not or do what you are unable to do, or should not do. "Stay in your lane!" For example, if you have the gift of being an assertive prophet, which means you are verbally expressive, you make quick judgments, you are often very direct, sometimes painfully, then leave the job of counseling to the one who is patient and has a heart for listening. If you are a generous giver, then let the job of treasurer be done by one who has the gift of administration, lest you give away all the church's money.

The solution is that all believers who have been baptized by the Holy Spirit have a gift to be used for the upbuilding of the Church of Christ. I might add that many are blessed with more than one gift. So, before you start grumbling about all the things you must do or talking about Bro. Joe or Sis. Mary for always being out front doing something, remember, it was Jesus who said (Luke 12:48b KJV) "For unto whomsoever much is given, of him shall be much required." Use your gifts. As in the parable of the talents found in Luke 19:11-24, "use it or lose it!"

Just as God put together our human bodies to function exactly right, God has put together the body of believers to function exactly right. Use the gifts God has given you McMichael! As we move forward through and beyond this pandemic, remember that it takes each one of us, through the guidance and empowerment of the Holy Spirit, for this body of believers to do and be what God has called us to be.

Pray, that while we are out with Covid-19, that God reveals to you the gifts and talents that have been placed in you to be used in McMichael. If it is teaching, then use this time to study God's Word and read books that give you additional insight into the Word of God, so that when we return, you will be able to give leadership in Christian Education. If it is intercessory prayer or showing mercy, call others, especially those who are ill or just need an encouraging word, and begin to develop an Intercessory Prayer Ministry. If giving, ask God to show you how you can be even more financially supportive of your church and how to develop a Stewardship Ministry. If it is administration, ask God to help you to develop a mission statement so that we as a body of believers can have a common focus for ministering to God's people. If exhortation, ask God to direct you to speak God's Word decently and in order, so that an Evangelism and Outreach Ministry can be developed.

My beloved brothers and sisters, we will get through this pandemic. And when we do come back, let us all come back swinging, truly being the church God is calling us to be. We are all essential workers in the Body of Christ.

1st Corinthians 12:12 NIV "*12 Just as a body, though one, has many parts, but all its many parts form one body, so it is with Christ. 13 For we were all baptized by one Spirit so as to form one body.'*

Let us pray: Loving God, I thank you for the gifts and talents you have given me. Help me to use them for the building up of your Kingdom here on earth and for the edification of my brothers and sisters. In Jesus name I pray, Amen.

THE CHURCH: GOD'S OWN

1st Peter 2:4-10

THE CHURCH! It's charter-the Bible; its foundation-the Cross; its mission -revival; it's power-the Holy Spirit; it's technique-faith; it's desire-worship; what makes it distinctive-love ("Love makes the difference"); its the structure-the body, and its results-Christianity.

The church is defined in two ways. We know that the church is a local assembly of believers who gather together to worship, study God's Word, and fellowship with one another. But more than that, THE CHURCH is defined as the redeemed of all ages, past and present, who follow Jesus Christ as Lord and Savior.

So now the question is, "What does it mean to be a member of THE CHURCH and a member of a particular church, such as McMichael AME Church?" Before we answer these questions, let us make sure we have a clear grasp of "what is the church?" The church is more than a building, a structure made of bricks and mortar, where people gather to worship on Sunday mornings or Wednesday night for Bible Study. During this season of the pandemic when church buildings have been closed, some feel that if you are not within the four walls of the building, then you are not in church. The fact that you are worshipping this morning on this worship service conference call lets me know that you understand the church is more than brick and mortar.

THE CHURCH, my brothers and sisters, is the people, you and me. THE CHURCH I am referring to is the believers who are on a continuous journey of spiritual growth, persons who are sincerely seeking and striving to be true disciples of Jesus Christ. THE CHURCH that I speak of is that universal body of redeemed saints who have repented of their sins, who have placed their faith and trust in Jesus Christ as their Lord and Savior, who are striving and intend to live according to God's Word, who are God-fearing and God-respecting believers, and whose true desire is to please God.

Understand that THE CHURCH is the means through which God ministers to God's people. We are God's hands and feet. God has a message of love and mercy, of judgment and grace, a message of forgiveness and salvation, and a message of hope that God wants the world to hear and accept. And it is the responsibility of THE CHURCH, through a church, that is you and me to proclaim these messages to a lost world.

Take note that I have said nothing about being a member of McMichael or the AME Church, or the Baptist Church, Full Gospel, Non-denominational, Church of God in Christ, United Methodist, Catholic (capital C) Presbyterian, Episcopal, or Seventh Day Adventist Church. For you see, being a member of THE CHURCH transcends and goes beyond individual churches and denominations. Being a member of THE CHURCH is about being in a relationship with God through God's Son Jesus Christ.

Follow me now. To be a committed, effective member of a church, that is McMichael or any other church, we must first understand what it means to be a member of THE CHURCH. It is possible to be a member of a church without being a member of THE CHURCH. What are you saying Rev. Pat? I am saying there are those in churches who are merely playing church, going through the motions. They know the right things to say, and even the right things to do. However, they are not in a relationship with God through Jesus Christ. They have the facade or front of being Christ-like, but in reality, they are not. And that is reflected in their lives, in the way they carry themselves and present themselves in their daily lives. What is truly in the heart is reflected by their words and actions.

One of the main images of the church used in the New Testament is "the people of God." Peter, who was Christ's main disciple to the Jews, used this term to instruct and encourage the Lord's disciples who had been scattered abroad, mainly because of being persecuted for being believers. Going back to the scripture that was read, the 9th verse *reads* (1st Peter 2:9 NKJV) *"But you are a chosen generation, a royal priesthood, a holy nation,*

His own special people, that you may proclaim the praises of Him who called you out of darkness into His marvelous light;"

First of all, understand that we are a chosen people. On the Day of Pentecost, God, through the power of the Holy Spirit identified 120 disciples, descendants of Abraham, Isaac, and Jacob, who had gathered in an upper room. Acts 2:2 KJV lets us know that as the *"…sound of a mighty rushing wind came down from heaven…"*, God breathed the Holy Spirit into these disciples that they would become the living Body of Christ. It was in this miraculous act that God was announcing to the Jewish nation that Jesus of Nazareth was indeed the Messiah, the Son of God. These 120 became the foundation of the new Israel, the people through whom God would carry God's redemptive ministry into the world. They were now the new people of God, the new chosen people through whom God would do God's work. It was on this foundation that the church grew.

As the spiritual descendants of Abraham, Isaac, and Jacob, and believers in Jesus Christ, we too are God's chosen people, chosen to carry the message of God's grace and mercy, the message of the love of Jesus Christ, and the empowering message of the Holy Spirit into the world.

Second, we are a "royal priesthood." Exodus 19:6 NKJV tells us that through Moses, God told the people of Israel *"And you shall be to Me a kingdom of priest and holy nation."* This passage proclaims the priesthood of every believer, and the responsibility of every believer to help unbelievers come to know God in and through Jesus Christ. We are to (1st Peter 2:9b NIV) *"declare the praises of Him who called you out of darkness* (sin) *into His wonderful light."* Tell others how Jesus freed you from that addiction, provided for you when you were down to nothing, how God made a way out of no way. And if this is not your testimony, you can simply testify to the fact that God woke you up to see another day. As the people of God, as believers in Jesus Christ, we are to be the instruments for taking God's message of love and grace to our needy world. We are the ones through whom an unsaved world, our unsaved family members, our unsaved friends will be drawn to the Lord Jesus Christ. Hymn writer Johnson Oatman put it this way.

How to reach the masses, those of every birth,
For and answer Jesus gave the key,
And I, if I be lifted up from the earth,
I'll draw all [persons] unto me.

[How do we do that?]
Lift Him up by living as a Christian ought,
Let the world in you the Savior see; [and then what happens?]
Then all will gladly follow Him who once taught,
I'll draw all [persons] unto me.

As believers, as members of the Body of Christ, we all have a responsibility, not just the pastor, not just the preachers, but all of us. We all have a responsibility to be an instrument through whom a nonbeliever can become acquainted with, witness, and experience, through our words and our actions, what it means to be in a relationship with God through God's Son Jesus Christ, and the saving grace of Jesus Christ. They should see the joy we have in serving a true and living God.

Next, we are a "holy nation." God told the people of Israel (Lev. 11:45 NIV) *"For I am the Lord who brought you out of the Land of Egypt, to be your God; you shall therefore be holy, for I am holy."* And then in addressing the church in Ephesus, Paul wrote (Eph 1:4 NIV) *"For He chose us in Him before the creation of the world to be holy and blameless in his sight,"*

As a spiritual babe, when I used to hear the word holiness, I thought of the Pentecostal or sanctified church. I thought of people shouting and "getting happy," speaking in tongues, dancing up and down the aisles, and being slain in the spirit. I believed that if you did not do these things, then you were not saved.

But, as I matured spiritually, I realized that this was not what holiness was about. I thank God for opening my eyes and spirit to the truth. Holiness, my brothers and sisters, is living by God's righteous nature and code of ethics. This past Wednesday in Bible Study, we discussed God's code of ethics, which is righteousness and holiness. Holiness is growing into the likeness of Christ and being consecrated, set aside for God's use. Understand my brothers and sisters, we are different from the world. The KJV says we are a peculiar (strange, unique, odd, distinctive) people. We belong to God, which makes us different from the world. How so? Again, in Wednesday night's Bible Study, the lesson was "Love Your Enemies." We read and discussed that when Jesus came down from the mountain after choosing his twelve disciples, he told the masses, (Luke 6:27 NIV) *"But I tell you who hear me; Love your enemies, do good to those who hate you, bless those who curse you, pray for those who mistreat you."* When confronted with these types of situations, our natural or worldly tendency is to retaliate. We had a very lively sharing on these and the following verse about "turning the other cheek."

What Christ was teaching them and us, was and is, a radical and courageous kind of love. In calling us to a life of holiness, God is calling us to be different from the world. People should be able to tell we are different in our walk, our talk, our reactions, our integrity, and most of all by our love. It is the love of Christ that makes the difference and that which makes us different! They should 'know we are Christians by our love."

Whether dressed in a business suit, an evening gown, a uniform, or a pair of jeans full of holes, an old t-shirt, and a baseball cap turned backward, when Christ is the center of your life, as God's peculiar people, as members of THE CHURCH, others will just know that you belong to Christ. You are so filled with the love and grace of God, that you cannot hide it even if you wanted to.

My beloved brothers and sisters in Christ, God has called us to be a chosen people, a royal priesthood, a holy nation, God's own special peculiar people. Why has God done this? So that by the way we represent God and Jesus Christ in our lives, others may come to know of the saving grace of Jesus Christ in the pardoning of their sins, that they may accept Jesus Christ as the Lord and Savior of their lives, and that they will know and understand that (John 3:16 KJV) *"God so loved the world, that he gave his only begotten Son, that whosoever believeth in him should not perish, but have everlasting life."*

I extend an invitation for you to become a member of THE CHURCH. Whether you are accepting Jesus Christ into your heart for the first time, whether you were a member of a church and left, and know it's just time for you to come back home, if you are coming from another church and choose to unite with the McMichael Church family, or even if you have been in a church all your life, and realize that you've never really been a part of THE CHURCH, I ask that you make yourself known today. You can call or text me. But please know, that it is not about being a member of a church, but it is about being a member of THE CHURCH, that is my beloved brothers and sisters, being in the right relationship with God through Jesus Christ, and allowing your life to be empowered by the abiding presence and guidance of the Holy Spirit.

Let us pray: Eternal and loving God, through your Holy Spirit, help me to be in right relationship with so that I will be a member of THE CHURCH. In the name of the Father, the Son, and the Holy Spirit, Amen.

WHAT'S IN YOUR CUP?

Matthew 12:34-37

The other day, I came across an interesting and very thought-provoking post on Facebook. Those of you who frequent Facebook might have seen the post. It went something like this. You are holding a cup of coffee when someone bumps into you and causes you to spill your coffee everywhere. The question is asked, "Why did you spill your coffee?" And of course, the response is "Because someone bumped into me!" Nope! Wrong answer! You spilled the coffee because coffee was in the cup. Had there been tea, milk, or any other liquid in the cup, that is what would have spilled. The point was whatever is in the cup is what will spill out. To put this in theological terms, whatever is in the heart will spill out.

Let us apply this concept to ourselves as written in the Word of God. Jesus had just healed a demon-possessed man who was also blind and deaf, and he was being confronted by the Pharisees. The religious leaders were refusing to believe that Jesus was from God and were accusing him of being in "cahoots" with satan. Jesus told them, as recorded in Matthew 12:34-37 NKJV *34) Brood of vipers! How can you, being evil, speak good things? For out of the abundance of the heart the mouth speaks. 35 A good man out of the good treasure of his heart brings forth good things, and an evil man out of the evil treasure brings forth evil things. 36 But I say to you that for every idle word men may speak, they will give account of it in the day of judgment. 37 For by your words you will be justified, and by your words you will be condemned."* The Message translation puts it like this. *34-37 "You have minds like a snake pit! How do you suppose what you say is worth anything when you are so foul-minded? It's your heart, not the dictionary, that gives meaning to your words. A good person produces good deeds and words season after season.*

An evil person is a blight on the orchard. Let me tell you something: Every one of these careless words is going to come back to haunt you. There will be a time of Reckoning. Words are powerful; take them seriously. Words can be your salvation. Words can also be your damnation."

Despite appearing to be "holier than Thou," the Pharisees were expressing what was really in their heart. It was at this point Jesus called them a brood of vipers and asked (Matthew 12:34 NIV) *"You brood of vipers, how can you who are evil say anything good? For the mouth speaks what the heart is full of"*

Luke also had something to say about what is in the heart. Luke 6:45 NKJV reads: *"A good man out of the good treasure of his heart brings forth good; and an evil man out of the evil treasure of his heart brings forth evil. For out of the abundance of the heart his mouth speaks.* The Living Bible says it this way- *"A good man produces good deeds from a good heart. And an evil man produces evil deeds from his hidden wickedness. Whatever is in the heart overflows into speech."*

In this Luke passage, Jesus is teaching about fruit in lives of people. He is saying that a good tree cannot bear bad fruit, and conversely, a bad tree cannot bear good fruit. Each tree is recognized by its fruit. In other words, that which is stored in the heart, good or bad, is revealed by what the mouth speaks.

When life happens, when "stuff" transpires that shakes you up, and trust me, it will, whatever is in your heart will come out. It is easy for us to put on a front and wear our masks to make it seems like we are as good as gold. But, when something comes along that rattles us, something that rocks the very foundation of our world, what comes out? That rocking can be as devastating as the loss of a loved one or being hospitalized for a month with COVID-19. It can be the weariness of being sheltered in place for the past two months or going to the store not being able to find the goods and supplies that are needed to help keep you and your loved ones safe. It can be someone cutting you off in traffic, or even someone bumping into you causing you to spill whatever is in your cup. How do you respond?

In the two passages of scripture that were shared, Jesus is reminding us that what we say reveals what is in our hearts. The good impressions we try to make will not last if our hearts are deceptive. Our words reveal our true underlying beliefs, attitudes, and motives. For our hearts to be cleansed, we must allow the Holy Spirit to fill us with new attitudes and motives. Then our speech will be cleansed at the source, which is our heart. What kind of words comes from your mouths?

James has a lot to say about the tongue, which is an instrument of the heart. Chap. 3:9-10 NIV says [9]*"With the tongue we praise our Lord and Father, and with it we curse men, who have been made in God's likeness.* [10]*Out of the same mouth come praise and cursing. My brothers [and sisters], this should not be."*

Remember the words of the Psalmist David who prayed (51:10 KJV) *"Create in me a clean heart, O God, and renew a right spirit within me."* And then Solomon wrote (Proverbs 4:23 NIV) *"Above all else, guard your heart, for it is the wellspring [the source,] of life."*

With this COVID-19, we are all under some type of stress, and that stress can come out through what we say and how we say things. Let us be mindful of how we talk to one another. Let us work toward filling our cups, our hearts with God's love, peace, compassion, kindness, forgiveness, words of affirmation. And then, "May the words of [our mouths], and the meditations of [our hearts,] be acceptable in God's sight, [our] strength and [our] redeemer. I ask the questions, "What is in your cup? What is in your heart?

Let us pray: Loving God, let what comes out of my mouth, which is a reflection of what is in my heart, be acceptable to you." In Jesus name I pray, Amen.

YOU CAN GET WITH THIS, OR YOU CAN GET WITH THAT!

Proverbs 9:10-12 James 3:13-18

A couple of years ago, I preached a sermon based on Joshua 24:15 NKJV which reads *"And if it seems evil to you to serve the Lord, choose for yourselves this day whom you will serve, whether the gods which your fathers served that were on the other side of the River, or the gods of the Amorites, in whose land you dwell. But as for me and my house, we will serve the Lord."* The title of that sermon was "You Can Get With This, Or You Can Get With That!" Well, this morning, I'm using that same title, but from a different perspective. I am looking at it from the standpoint of wisdom, two types of wisdom, one that comes from God, and the other that comes from the world.

Proverbs has a lot to say a lot about wisdom, and the choices we make. It tells us that if we live wisely, according to the guidelines outlined in the Word of God, then we receive blessings from God. If we choose to live foolishly, according to the world's standards, and follow our own stubborn path, then we can expect regret, pain, and destruction. In other words, we can get with this, or we can get with that. And then James 3:13-18 also tells us that there are two types of wisdom. There is heavenly wisdom that comes from God, and then there is earthly wisdom that comes from the world. Again, we can get with this, or we can get with that!

Let us take a closer look at these two wisdoms, where they come from, their nature, and their fruits. We know that heavenly wisdom comes from God. This type of wisdom comes through studying God's Word, prayer, and being in the right relationship with God. James 1:5 NIV says, *"If any of you lack wisdom, [you] should ask God, who gives generously to all without finding fault. And it will be given to [you]."* So, even if we've been following the earthly standards of the world and have gotten caught up in the temptations of the world, if we ask God for God's wisdom, God will give it. But as vs. 6 says, we must ask believing, and without doubt.

Heavenly wisdom leads to peace and justice. James 3:17-18 NIV reads *"17 But the wisdom that comes from above is first of all pure, then peace-loving, considerate, submissive, full of mercy and good fruit, impartial, and sincere. 18 Peacemakers who sow in peace raise a harvest of righteousness.* God's heavenly wisdom enables us to apply Godly wisdom to life's challenges. When faced with problems at home, on the job, in school, applying God's wisdom of peace, love, and compassion will help to see us through. When we apply heavenly wisdom to our lives, personal conflicts will be less, and harmonious relations will grow. Having Godly wisdom creates spiritual integrity within our mind, heart, and spirit, which frees us from the jealousies, envy, and self-ambitions that come from earthly wisdom. It gives us a peaceful, gentle, and non-judgmental spirit. Again, this type of wisdom comes through having the Word of God in our heart, mind, and spirit, through prayer, and being in the right relationship with God. The Psalmist David wrote (Psalm 119:11 KJV) *"Thy Word have I hid in my heart, that I may not sin against thee."* He also wrote, (Psalm 51:10 NIV) *"Create in me a clean heart, and renew a right spirit within me."* Know my brothers and sisters, that you can choose to "get with this!"

Now, let's look at earthly wisdom, that which comes from the world. Earthly wisdom appeals to the senses, emotions, and passions of our being. It is all about what feels good and what feels right. Its influence comes from the devil and the devil's followers. When the flesh and satan combine to pull us into worldly wisdom, it causes disharmony and chaos in our lives, and our relationships. James 1:14-15(AMP) tells us *14 But each one is tempted when he is dragged away, enticed and baited [to commit sin] by his own [worldly] desire (lust, passion). 15 Then when the illicit desire has conceived, it gives birth to sin; and when sin has run its course, it gives birth to death.*

Worldly wisdom my brothers and sisters, is full of envy and is self-seeking. This type of wisdom causes confusion, conflict, chaos, and trouble, at home, on the job, in the classroom, and yes, even in the church. Worldly wisdom comes from jealously and self-ambition that dwells in the heart. Luke 6:45b (NRSV) states *"...and the evil person out of evil treasure produces evil: for it is out of the abundance of the heart that the mouth speaks."* Worldly wisdom lifts the merits of power, privilege, position, and prestige. This sounds like someone presently residing at 1600 Pennsylvania Ave. in Washington, DC., whose number is 45. (And I might add, that if we do not get out and vote on November 3rd, he will continue to reside there.) It is this earthly wisdom that causes one to rebel against God, and to seek their own way. It was this type of wisdom, the seeking of power and position that caused satan to be thrown out of heaven.

Earthly wisdom leads to wars, both foreign and domestic. It caused Dylan Roof to go into Mother Emanuel AME Church, and kill nine persons in a Bible Study. He intended to start a race war. Earthly wisdom leads to injustice and allows rogue white police officers to kill unarmed black men and women, such as George Floyd, Breonna Taylor, Jacob Blake, and closer to home, Lafayette resident Trayford Pellerin, who was shot over 10 times by the police. The injustice of worldly wisdom is what allowed a mother to drive her 17-year-old son, with a loaded rifle, to the Jacob Blake demonstration in Kenosha, Wisconsin, and openly kill two demonstrators. He was then able to walk by several police vehicles with the open weapon, to go home, enjoy a meal, and then get arrested.

It is this type of wisdom that causes a person to try to climb to the top, whatever and wherever that is, and who will squash anyone that gets in his or her way, causes them to feel threatened, and who will steal, kill, and destroy to get their way. The TV show American Greed is a real eye-opener. The entertainment industry thrives on these types of scenarios with shows like Suits, Have and Have Nots, and Empire. My brothers and sisters, if you so choose, you can get with that!

Now knowing the two types of wisdom that are before us, you can choose heavenly wisdom which leads to life with our heavenly Father through Jesus Christ and be led by the Holy Spirit, or you can choose to follow the standards of the world and live a life that is led by the devil and his followers. In other words, my brothers and sisters, "You Can Get with This, or You Can Get with Can Get with That!" The choice is yours. If you choose THIS, know that the road will not be easy. But when we commit our lives to God through God's Son Jesus Christ, and allow ourselves to be led by the Holy Spirit, when we consciously pursue heavenly wisdom, when we remain faithful to Jesus Christ, then we can stand on God's promise that, as written by the prophet Isaiah who foretold of the coming of the Messiah, (Isaiah 41:10 NIV) *"So do not fear, for I am with you; do not be dismayed, for I am your God. I will strengthen you, and help you; I will uphold you with My righteous right hand."*

However, if on the other hand, you choose THAT, to live by the world's standards, I strongly urge you to change, to allow your heart to be converted and commit your life to Christ, so that in this life and eternity, rather than experiencing the wrath of God, you will be able to experience the love, joy, peace, and forgiveness that comes from being in relationship with God. My brothers and sisters, I strongly urge you to GET WITH THIS!

Let us pray: Dear God, giver of wisdom, let me be led by the Holy Spirit to make the right choice to follow Your Heavenly wisdom. Show me how to apply Your Godly wisdom when faced with life's challenges. In Jesus name I pray, Amen

WHAT IS REQUIRED?

Micah 6:6-8

In today's society, we tend to use the words love and hate so casually, that they have to a large degree, lost their true meaning. They have become society's catchphrases, clichés, thrown carelessly at objects, situations, and people. I love those shoes! I love watching football! Likewise, I hate having to practice, I hate the way she drives. Love and hate!

It is sometimes hard for us, as believers, to understand statements that describe a loving God who hates sin. We see God as a loving parent, a loving Father who is gentle and kind. That is who and what God is. However, our full perception and understanding of God are distorted, misleading, when we fail to recognize that God also does hate. What is it that God hates? God hates sin.

What is sin? (I am glad you asked!) Sin is an evil force. It is transgression and rebellion against the divine law of God. Sin had its beginning with satan, who was cast out of heaven because of the sin of pride, and who then, in the form of a serpent, caused Adam and Eve to sin. 1 John 3:4 NIV describes sin as lawlessness. *"Everyone who sins breaks the law; in fact, sin is lawlessness."* We know that God gave Moses The Ten Commandments, which is the Law of God. Sin is unbelief, making God a liar. It is foolishness to deceive you, and a force to destroy you. Sin, my brothers and sisters, is a volitional, intentional act of disobedience against the revealed will and Word of God.

Understand, God's hatred of sin is real. It is a burning consuming judgment that can and will destroy. God hates sin and stands as the righteous judge, ready to deal out just and fair punishment to those who defy, disobey God's laws.

Now, just as God's hate is real, so is God's love. It is so real, that God sent God's only begotten Son, Jesus Christ to save and accept judgment in the sinner's place, for your sins, and my sins. Love and hate are together, the flip sides of the same coin. I know Baby Boomers remember Luther Ingram's hit from the late 1960s, "There's a Thin Line Between Love and Hate." (There was also a movie by the same name starring Angela Basset and Martin Lawrence.)

In the short seven chapters of Micah, [which I encourage you to read] the prophet presents a true picture of God, the almighty God who hates sin and loves the sinner. Micah, which means "who is like Jehovah" was a younger contemporary of the great prophet Isaiah. As a prophet, Micah's love for God and his obedience to God would not allow him to offer false hopes to those who were under God's sentence of judgment. He told it like it was. He did not sugar-coat nor did he bite his tongue. Over and over again, Micah warned both nations of Judah and Israel of God's impending judgment because of their moral decay. Both nations had sunk to a depraved and decadent low that included fraud, debauchery, theft, oppression, hypocrisy, heresy, extortion, lying, and murder. Micah knew that God was going to use the Assyrian nation and army as an instrument of God's wrath and judgment, if the nations, the people did not repent and turn back to God.

Like a skilled attorney, Micah presented God's case against Judah and Israel, their leaders, and their people. The prophet made it clear that God despised, that God hated the injustice, lack of compassion, and disobedience to God that was going on.

As we look at our society today, we see injustice at almost every turn. We see the systemic injustice that goes from our ancestors being snatched from the Motherland, forced into chattel slavery, and the inhumane treatment they received. We see the injustice continuing after the Emancipation Proclamation and the rise of hate organizations like the Ku Klux Klan and the legalized injustice of Jim Crow laws. The Civil Rights Movement brought the injustices pressed upon African-Americans to the forefront. And those injustices continue with rogue police officers who literally get away with the murder of African-American men and women…in the name of the law. Today, I know God is not pleased!! You have those who believe the fires on the west coast, the pandemic, hurricanes are all God's way of getting our attention. God has got mine!

As we look at chapter 6, Micah creates the scene of a court trial-God vs. the People. Imagine yourself sitting in that courtroom. The plaintiff is God, whose speaker is Micah, and the defendants are the people, the nations of Israel and Judah. Why you may ask are the people on trial? Well, in addition to their moral decline, they had turned the worship of God into a ritual of outward show, a fancy display of just going through the motions. They no longer worshipped God from the heart.

Additionally, they had even gotten into worshipping and offering sacrifices to pagan gods. Through the prophet Micah, God tells them, as recorded in Micah 6:1 NIV, *"Stand up, plead your case before the mountains; let the hills hear what you have to say."* The Lord is calling on the mountains as witnesses for the prosecution because God knew the mountains would and could confirm Israel's and Judah's guilt. For it was on the high mountains, on high places that the people erected altars to pagan gods, offered sacrifices, and worshipped.

The plaintiff-God continues to present His case. Beginning with Micah 6:3 NIV, God asks *"What have I done to you? How have I burdened you? Answer me."* I sense that God has forgotten His role as the plaintiff and has slid into a parental role. It is the sound of a pleading parent who must rebuke and chastise his or her wayward child. "Why are you treating me like this?" Then God goes through a list of things that have been done for the nations. God reminds them that He brought them out of Egypt, gave them good leadership in Moses, Aaron, and Miriam, and gave them instructions on how to live when they entered the Promised Land. He brought up the fact that they had renewed their covenant with God. I can imagine, like a frustrated parent God saying "Why, my people, why? How can you forget the things I've done? Is your memory that short? Can you, my children (still claiming them) really be that thankless". Parents, grandparents, guardians! Does that sound familiar? The Lord, the prosecution then rests His case.

The room is so quiet that you could hear a pin drop. There's another phrase we use, but I won't. The people sit there with their heads bowed down, feeling very guilty and convicted. You know how you felt when your parents got on your case about something you had done and you knew you were wrong. The people of Israel and Judah knew, that not even the legal team of Thurgood Marshall, Johnnie Cochran, and Benjamin Crump could get them off.

Now, the attorney for the defense, speaking for Judah and Israel comes forward asking Micah, what can be done to please God, to get back in God's good graces. Micah 6:6-7 NIV reads *⁶"With what shall I come before the Lord and bow myself before the exalted Lord. Shall I come before Him with burnt offerings, with calves a year old?* I imagine Micah is sitting there stone-faced, totally without expression. The spokesperson continues by asking Micah 6:7 NIV *Will God be pleased with a thousand rams, with ten rivers of oil?* Still not being able to get any response from the prophet, he offers the ultimate sacrifice. *Shall I offer my firstborn for my transgression, the fruit of my body for the sin of my soul?"*

Before we go on, there's something to be said about the spokesperson. First of all, he recognized the sinfulness of himself and his people. He knew they needed to be reconciled to God. Secondly, he assumed that the only path back to God was through the ritual of sacrifice. It was his sincere desire for his people and himself to get right with God, but they didn't know how. He wanted Micah to tell him which sacrifice would be most effective.

In verse 8, Micah responds. He lets the spokesman know that he is totally missing the point, missing the heart of the matter. It was and is not about the rituals and sacrifice. It's not about being on the line every Sunday morning and Wednesday evening. It's not about receiving communion every first Sunday and praying seven times a day. Nor is it about reading your Bible morning, noon, and night. He tells him, and us (Micah 6:8 NIV) *⁸"He has showed you, O man, what is good. And what does the Lord require of you? To act justly, and to love mercy, and to walk humbly with your God."* What the Lord requires is so plain and simple, so simple that it's hard for some to understand. Let's take a look at each of these.

Justice is something we do. It's about causing and implementing change, setting right that which is wrong. It's about speaking truth to power, to the decision makers-those in government, those in authority, and leadership positions. It's about attending council meetings and making our voices heard. Justice means protecting the rights of the oppressed, the weak, and defenseless in our society and our communities. Justice means practicing the principles of fairness, honesty, and integrity in all of our dealing with others. Justice, my brothers and sisters, means making our voices heard by getting out there and voting on Tuesday, November 3rd. Amen!

The second requirement is to show kindness, loving-kindness to others. Kindness can be used to describe the key element in all relationships, whether with friendships, marriage, family, co-workers, classmates, neighbors, and in our relationship with God. It's loving someone more than is required of us. It's showing compassion to that wayward child who needs a strong word of encouragement and discipline. It's showing love to someone whose only claim to our love is the need to be loved. It's showing kindness to someone not because of who they are, or are not, but because of who we are, which is a child of God. It's demonstrating the kind of love God has for us, that is unconditional agape love.

Finally, we are to walk humbly with the Lord. This means putting God first in all that we do and allowing our lives to conform to the will of God. When we walk humbly with the Lord, we are in constant fellowship with God. We fellowship with God through prayer, reading, studying, and reflecting on God's Word, through praise and worship, and by being in fellowship with other believers. Luke 6:45b NKJV tells us *"For out of the abundance of the heart his mouth speaks."* Our talk, our walk, our actions, our thoughts should all reflect the presence of God in our lives.

My beloved brothers and sisters. Understand that the God we serve, the God we love, the God who constantly shows us love, kindness, compassion, grace, mercy, and forgiveness, is the same God who hates sin, and will bring wrath upon those who refuse to turn from their sinful ways. Where do you stand with God? If there is any doubt in your heart, mind, or spirit about being in the right relationship with God, then I suggest, strongly urge, beg you to begin by repenting, and turning from your sinful ways. The psalmist David wrote in Ps. 51:3-4 NIV [3]*"For I know my transgressions and my sin is ever before me. [4]Against you, and you only have I sinned, and done what is evil in your sight, so that you are proved right when you speak and justified when you judge."*

Know, my brothers and sisters, that God is a God of second chances. It is never too late to turn away from sin and turn to God. And then, if you have not accepted Christ as your Lord and personal Savior, do so today, right now. Know that Christ died on Calvary's cross for your sins, for my sins, for the sins of the whole world, so that we would not have to experience the judgmental wrath of God. Christ died to set us free from our sins, to give us new life, and to allow us to be in the right relationship with God.

My prayer for you my McMichael family is that you allow God, through His Son Jesus Christ, and through the power of the Holy Spirit to have control of your life, so that we can all experience the joy that comes from being a forgiven child of God, and the joy that comes from serving a true and living God. Let us go forth this day as children of God, knowing and doing what is required of us, that is to act justly, to love mercy, and to walk humbly with God.

Let us pray: Dear Lord, may my life reflect the justice, mercy, and humility that you require of me. Let others see You in me. In the name of the Father, the Son, and the Holy Spirit I pray, Amen.

LET'S GET IT RIGHT

1st Corinthians 1:17-29 (27-28)

As we prepare to celebrate and commemorate the broken body and shed blood of our Lord and Savior Jesus Christ through Holy Communion, just for a few moments, I would like to share from the thought "LET'S GET IT RIGHT."

There are two sacraments that we as Methodists observe-that is Baptism and Holy Communion. Communion, also known as the Lord's Supper, was established by Jesus Christ at the Passover meal that He shared with His beloved disciples including Judas, the night before His crucifixion.

The apostle Paul had a lot to say to the Corinthian church regarding this sacrament, and they were not pleasant. Paul had received reports that the communion, the Lord's Supper was becoming more of a spiritual hindrance to the members rather than a means of spiritual growth. Paul was deeply concerned over how the communion meal was being celebrated.

What was going on that had Paul so riled up, so aggravated? First of all, there were divisions and divisive attitudes among the believers. Let us back up to 1st Cor. 1:10-17 when Paul first began to get word as to what was really going on in the Corinthian church. Divisions had developed in the church regarding God's messengers. 1st Corinthians 1:10-12 NKJV reads
10 "Now I plead with you, brethren, by the name of our Lord Jesus Christ, that you all speak the same thing, and that there be no divisions among you, but that you be perfectly joined together in the same mind and in the same judgment. 11 For it has been declared to me concerning you, my brethren, by those of Chloe's household, that there are contentions among you. 12 Now I say this, that each of you says, "I am of Paul," or "I am of Apollos," or "I am of Cephas," or "I am of Christ."

What Paul was telling the members of the church is that Paul, Apollos, and Cephas were all on the same team, and not rivals. Even though there might be some differences in how they presented the Gospel, it was the same Gospel they were proclaiming. Paul's approach to the Gospel was based on his preaching to Gentiles, many of whom had little or no knowledge of the Hebrew Scripture. Jesus had taught and preached using parables and stories for the same reason. Apollos had to deal with Greek-speaking Jews called Hellenists, whose culture was steeped in philosophy, art, music, literature, and natural history. He also had to frame the Gospel in light of Jewish opposition. But he was preaching the same Gospel. They did not preach different gospels. There is one gospel adapted to the recipients of the message.

Now, back to the problem with Communion. The city of Corinth could be considered the Las Vegas or New Orleans of its day. People came to Corinth to participate in the gambling, legalized prostitution, amusements, and business adventures this city had to offer. There was a lack of moral standards that prevailed in the city.

Those who settled in this city were the ones who through the powerful preaching and teaching of Paul, eventually made up the Corinthian Church. Despite their differences, they had to learn to live and worship in harmony with one another.

Now the tradition was that before communion was administered, there was an agape meal or love feast. This was an opportunity for members of the congregation to come together to eat and fellowship with one another before receiving the Lord's Supper. This followed the example set by Christ when he shared the Passover meal with his disciples.

Remember now, you have folks from all walks of life in the church-rich and poor, learned and unlearned, Gentiles and Jews. As human nature would have it, there began to be a line drawn between those who were well off and those who lacked, the have and have nots. Naturally, those who could afford it, brought the food, supposedly to be shared by everyone. Unfortunately, the less fortunate members of the congregation were being left out of taking part in the agape meal. Paul also received word that some were eating excessively and getting drunk. Paul had already dealt with division and divisive attitudes in the congregation caused by members aligning themselves with the different preachers. And now he knew he had to straighten out the situation dealing with the Love Feast and Communion.

He saw that the members were losing their understanding of the true spiritual essence and significance of these rituals. He told the church (1ˢᵗ Corinthians 11:17-18 NIV) *"¹⁷ In the following directives, I have no praise for you, for your meetings do more harm than good. ¹⁸ In the first place, I hear that when you come together as a church, there are divisions among you, and to some extent, I believe it.* Now it sounds to me that Paul was quite upset with them.

Regarding the Agape meal, this was supposed to be a time when the members could come together to break bread in fellowship and love and to spiritually prepare themselves to *worthily* receive the Lord's Supper. The broken bread offered by Christ to his disciples, including Judas, was a final earthly act of forgiving love on the part of Christ. Wouldn't it be great if we would show that same type of forgiving love to one another? Wouldn't it be wonderful if we could put aside our differences, and focus on our relationship with God, and with one another?

Wouldn't it be wonderful if we could truly be forgiving…and be forgiven? Just think of the spiritual growth that would take place in our lives, both individually and as a church body if we all came to Love Feast, to spiritually prepare our hearts and spirits to participate in the Lord's Supper, to kneel at the communion rails in your hearts, and know that we have reconciled ourselves with each other, and most importantly, with God

Paul goes on to instruct the Corinthian church on the correct way to conduct the Communion service as given to him by the Lord. He states (1ˢᵗ Corinthians 11:27 NIV) *²⁷"Therefore, whoever eats the bread or drinks the cup of the Lord in an unworthy manner will be guilty of sinning against the body and the blood of the Lord."* When he said in an unworthy manner, he was referring to church members who would rush in and receive communion without really thinking about its meaning. Instead of honoring the sacrifice of Jesus Christ, their hearts and minds are elsewhere,

Again, Paul is trying to get the Corinthian church members to understand the true magnitude of the Lord's Supper. It is not a meaningless ritual that we observe each first Sunday, but a sacrament given to us by Jesus Christ to strengthen our faith. Even though, because of the pandemic we are worshipping together through technology, and sharing in the communion virtually, the spiritual significance remains the same.

Christ died on that old, rugged cross, and bore the sins of the whole world so that we could be forgiven and reconciled to the heavenly Father. Christ suffered, bled, and died. The songwriter Kenneth Louis put it this way:

"Just for me, just for me.
Just for me, just for me.
They pierced Him in His side,
He hung his head and died.
He did all that, just for me."

As we prepare to receive the elements which represent the body and blood of Jesus Christ, just for a moment, reflect on what Jesus Christ did for you and me. Pray for the Holy Spirit to dwell in your heart and spirit so that you may worthily receive his body and blood.

My brothers and sisters, if Jesus Christ died just for you, for me, for the whole world, how can we repay him for the gift of his sacrifice? We can do so by receiving the bread and wine with love and thanksgiving in our hearts, thanking God for His Son Jesus Christ who came into the world to show us how to love one another. We can do so by accepting Jesus Christ as our Lord and Savior, by living our lives for Him, by sharing the good news of serving a true and living God, and loving one another, as Jesus taught us to love.

Let us pray: Loving God, let me live my life in such a way that Jesus' death on the cross was not in vain. In the precious name of Jesus I pray, Amen.

A REASON TO REJOICE

Romans 5:1-11

Some years ago, gospel recording artist Kirk Franklin recorded a song entitled "The Reason Why I Sing." Part of the lyrics are *"Someone asked the question, why do we sing, when we lift our hands to Jesus, what does it really mean?"* The response is *"I sing because I'm happy, I sing because I'm free, His eye is on the sparrow, that's the reason why I sing."*

The Baton Rouge Advocate has a daily feature called Today's Thought which is a Bible verse and a thought related to the verse. To show you how God works, yesterday's thought was Ephesians 5:19-20 NIV. It reads [19] *Speaking to one another with psalms, hymns, and songs from the Spirit. Sing and make music from your heart to the Lord,* [20] *always giving thanks to God the Father for everything, in the name of our Lord Jesus Christ.* G.E. Dean, author of Dean's Guide to the Bible wrote "Christians have a reason to sing. We are saved from sin and filled with thanksgiving for what He has done in us." This thought is so relevant to this morning's message,

Today, I'm putting a twist on the question by asking "Why do we rejoice?" I'm twisting it even more by asking, "How can we rejoice? How can we rejoice in midst of this COVID-19 pandemic, which has turned our lives, our day-to-day living as we have known it, upside down and inside out?

From the scripture that was read, we can find our answers. One such answer is the concept of righteousness, which is very much a part of the fiber of Romans. Righteousness is simply holy and upright living according to God's standards. Therefore, our righteousness is defined in terms of God's righteousness.

I know someone is asking what does righteousness have to do with rejoicing. Well, some of the most excited people are those who recently

42

became Christian. They are experiencing a joy they did not have before, because they realize that God has taken away their sins, lifted their burden of guilt, and given them a new life in Christ. Unfortunately, what happens for some is that somewhere along their Christian journey, they lose their excitement, their enthusiasm over being saved.

It is like seeing the difference in the excitement of a young, or older couple falling in love, and a couple that has been together for many years. The love is still there, but the giddiness of being in love has diminished. You know what I am talking about. It is wonderful to see that couple, especially an elderly couple that has been together for many years still being "silly" about being in love.

So it is with us as Christians. It is refreshing and uplifting to see a mature Christian, and I'm not necessarily talking about mature in age, to see a mature Christian who is still excited about being saved, one who has not lost that original thrill and gratitude for God saving them from the power, penalty, punishment, and guilt of their sins.

Paul wrote this letter to the Roman Church many years after his conversion on the Damascus Road. He was still overflowing with joy. What was it after all these years, through the many trials and tribulations he experienced, like being shipwrecked, persecuted, beaten, even left for dead that allowed him to still have that joy? After all Paul had been through, what was the reason that Paul was still able to rejoice in the Lord? His reasons for rejoicing, my brothers and sisters, are the same reasons we should have.

First of all, Paul remembered. He remembered how depraved and treacherous his past was. He remembered that before his Damascus Road experience, he was a notorious persecutor of the followers of Christ. He would have them jailed, even killed. Remember, Paul was a Pharisee, a devout Jew who sincerely believed that the followers of "The Way" were a threat to the sanctity of Judaism. Paul remembered his past.

I'm sure that if we look at our own past, we can say "thank you Lord for saving me!" In talking with and sharing our life's story with young people, they need to know that "we ain't always been saved." We did some "stupid stuff" and were knuckleheads. But...it was, and is by God's grace and mercy, that in spite of God seeing us in those conditions, when we were in what I call "the ozone period" of our lives, when we repented and asked God for forgiveness, God loved us enough to forgive us and save us. When you think of where God has brought you from, that in and of itself is a reason to rejoice. Rejoice, my brothers and sisters.

Secondly, we have a reason to rejoice when we recognize the depth of God's love for us. Romans 5:8 NKJV reads, *"God demonstrated his own love toward us, in that while we were yet sinners, Christ died for us."* Know my brothers and sisters, that we cannot out-sin God's grace and mercy. Let that marinate for a moment. Again, know that we cannot out-sin God's grace and mercy. When we think that the one who created us, the one who knows us best, the one who knows all our faults and shortcomings, the one who knows those secrets we try to hide from one another, we cannot hide them from God. When we think about the one who gave His only begotten Son to die on the cross for us while we were yet sinners, how can we not rejoice? We should be jumping for joy all over the place, recognizing the depth of God's love for you and me.

Finally, the way for us to maintain that joy is to realize the growth that God intends for us. There is so much more to this Christian journey than a one-time decision to follow Christ. That is just the beginning. It is an exciting journey that begins with the first step of receiving Christ into your heart and accepting Him as Lord, that is turning over your life and trusting your life to Christ, and accepting Christ as your Savior, that is understanding and believing that Christ died for your sins. That growth comes when we commit ourselves to reading, studying, meditating, reflecting upon, and then applying God's Word to our lives. Knowledge is knowing…wisdom is doing. During this time of sheltering in place, take the time to spend quality time with the Lord. Pray, seriously pray every day. Continue to worship and fellowship together as a church family Wednesday evenings and Sunday mornings via conference calls. We may not be that advanced technically, but we are still able to come together to praise and worship the Lord and to fellowship and encourage one another during these challenging times. This is our reason to rejoice.

My brothers and sisters! Think about your past and where God has brought you from. REJOICE! Recognize how deep God's love is for you. REJOICE! Know that you are on an exciting journey of spiritual growth, striving for the righteousness of God! REJOICE in the Lord always, again I say rejoice!

Rejoice in the Lord always, again I say rejoice.
Rejoice in the Lord always again I say rejoice.
Rejoice, rejoice, again I say rejoice;
Rejoice, rejoice, again I say rejoice
(Sing as a round!)

Let us pray: Lord God, as I continue to grow in you, let me never lose my excitement of being a child of the Most High. Let me rejoice in You, always! In the joyful name of Jesus I pray, Amen

ASSURANCE-TRUST

PERFECT PEACE

Isaiah 26:3

We know that life in and of itself is not perfect. All of us have situations in our lives that cause our lives to be imperfect. It can be financial and economic, family circumstances, individual health issues, and of course, what we all are experiencing right now, COVID-19, the coronavirus.

Our lives, our routines, our coming and going have all been drastically changed due to this worldwide epidemic. The way we do life has been seriously altered. I do not need to go into detail about how much this has impacted our lives because we all know firsthand. The fact that we are worshipping the way we are this morning is indicative of the changes we have had to make in our lives.

Isaiah 26:3 KJV reads *"Thou wilt keep him in perfect peace, whose mind is stayed on thee: because he trusteth in thee."* It is plain that "perfect peace" is not dependent on the circumstances and situations that surround our lives. Understand, perfect peace is not about the absence of bad circumstances, but about the reassuring presence of God, despite the circumstance. God's peace comes to us amid our most difficult and challenging times.

When we think too much about tomorrow, and even today-will I contract the virus, have I been exposed, do I have enough food if I must be quarantined, will I have a job, where can I find hand sanitizer, toilet paper, and bread, how long will I have to stay in the house, when will this madness end? When we think too much about the problems and challenges we are facing, we can easily become worried and anxious and take our minds off of God. Instead of peace, we experience anxiety and turmoil.

The secret to having perfect peace, my brothers and sisters comes when our focus is on God and not on the challenging and difficult circumstances in which we find ourselves. Isaiah 26:3 AMP says*"You will keep in perfect and constant peace the one whose mind is steadfast [that is, committed and focused on You—in both inclination and character], because he trusts and takes refuge in You [with hope and confident expectation]."*

Perfect peace, my brothers and sisters, comes when our minds are "stayed on thee." It is about trusting God. It is about standing on the promises of God, whom we know is a promise keeper. Trusting in God comes from knowing God, from being in relationship with God. And that relationship comes about through prayer, reading, studying, and meditating on God's Word, and from being in fellowship with like-minded believers. I might add, this is an excellent time to seriously spend time in family worship, reading God's Word, and praying together as a family

As we continue in these uncharted waters of the virus, we must remain focused on God. As songwriter Ian Stanphill wrote,

"Many things about tomorrow,
I don't seem to understand.
But I know who holds tomorrow,
and I know who holds my hand."

And yes, there are many things we don't understand. Even though we all probably have our theories, 2nd Chronicles 7:14 NIV does come to mind:" ***If*** *My people who are called by My name will humble themselves, and pray and seek My face, and turn from their wicked ways,* **then** *I will hear from heaven, and will forgive their sin and heal their land."* Despite the sinfulness of our country, we can still have the peace of knowing that God will see us through. The writer of Hebrews wrote (Hebrews 13:5 NIV) *"For He Himself has said, 'I will never leave you nor forsake you"*

My beloved brothers and sisters, don't lose heart. We will get through this together. It is so important for us to remain connected, remain in contact with one another so we can encourage one another, lift one another's spirits, share our thoughts and our fears. Yes, even though we are putting our trust in God, God knows what we are experiencing emotionally and mentally because God made us as human beings with feelings. Support one another. Call one another just to see how others are doing. For those who utilize social media, send positive messages to one another. When you receive an uplifting message, share it.

Paul wrote to the Philippian church (4:6-7 NIV) *"Do not be anxious for anything, but in everything, by prayer, and petition, with thanksgiving, present your request to God. (7) And the peace of God, which transcends all understanding, will guard your hearts and your minds in Jesus Christ."*

My brothers and sisters, know that (Isaiah 26:3-4 CEV) *"³The Lord gives perfect peace to those whose faith is firm. ⁴ So always trust the Lord because he is forever our mighty rock."*

Let us pray: God of peace, regardless of my circumstance, help me to keep my focus on You, so that I may have that perfect peace that only comes from being in relationship with you. In the name of the Father, the Son, and the Holy Spirit I pray, Amen.

WHAT WILL GET US THROUGH?

Psalm 23

(based on Meditation by Rev. Garland Pierce- AME
Department of Christian Education)

One of the most familiar and beloved passages of scripture many of us learned as children alongside the Lord's Prayer, one that even non-believers know or are at least familiar with, a passage of scripture we can recite by rote, is the beloved 23rd Psalm. This Psalm is one that brings us much comfort and assurance.

Familiarity itself has a way of bringing about comfort. We are familiar with the routines we have established of waking in the morning, preparing for work or school, of eating at certain times. We are familiar with the streets and roads we travel to get to where we must go. There is a familiarity of going to the grocery store and buying basic household items and food. Knowing how we are going to do things gives us a sense of security and comfort.

So much that has been familiar to us has now changed. These past few weeks have been anything but familiar. We have been hearing and learning words and terms like flattening the curve, shelter in place, self-quarantine and self-isolation, social distancing, "new normal," pandemic, and the one I had to look up, <u>mitigation</u>, meaning curbing the spread of the virus.

With so much change going on in our lives these days, let us draw our attention to something familiar. That my brothers and sisters is the 23rd Psalm. In this health crisis, we are looking for competent, reliable leadership from our governmental, health, community, and church leaders. In our looking, remember that "the Lord is our shepherd." Yes, the Lord has placed in our midst, medical experts, and organizations such as the CDC and World Health Organization to keep us abreast of the situation, who let us know what we should and should not be doing to try to curb this pandemic, who provides us with information we can trust. I applaud our governor for the information he and his staff provide. But know, it is the Lord our Shepherd, in whom we are to place our ultimate trust.

For those wondering what to do in times like these, remember (Psalm 23:2a NSRV). *"He leads us beside the still waters"* Last week I spoke about perfect peace. We have to be still, quiet ourselves so we can hear from God. We must pray and reflect on God's Word. In that quietness, the Lord will reveal to us how to apply God's word to our lives and the situations we are experiencing.

To those who are sick, stressed out with worry, and just tired of everything, the words (23:3a NSRV) *"he restores my soul"* come to mind. We are being bombarded each waking hour with the numbers of those who have contracted the virus and the number of those who have died. However, know that many have been healed and are doing well. Even though the numbers seem high, there are a lot more surviving the virus than the media releases to the public. I have my theory on that, which has to do with inciting fear in our hearts. But just know that (2nd Timothy 1:7 NSRV) *"God has not given us a spirit of fear, but a spirit of power, love, and a sound mind [self-discipline/common sense].* Let us praise God for those who have been cured and released from the hospitals.

To those on the frontlines, the first responders, the healthcare professionals, especially the nurses and Certified Nursing Assistants-CNAs, those who work in the grocery stores, the Dollar Generals, fast food and carry-out restaurants, service stations, banks, the ones who are risking their health to keep things as normal as possible, I praise and thank God for them. Some have even tested positive and are sick. To them the psalmist says (Psalm 23:4a NKJV) *"Yea though I walk through the valley of the shadow of death, I will fear no evil."* For me, the operative word in this stanza is "through," meaning I going in, but I'm coming out on the other side. It does not say Yea thou I walk through the valley and get stuck! It means that even though I am going through this trying time, this time of uncertainty, this time of illness, this time of challenge, I know that the Lord, who is my shepherd, will lead me out.

For those who have lost loved ones, and not necessarily only related to the virus, those who are unable to traditionally celebrate the life of their loved one, the words (Psalm 23:4b NSRV) *"for you are with me. Your rod and staff they comfort me."* These words are there to bring comfort to the hearts of those left behind.

Then, there are those who are abused and are not able to have a safe distance from their abuser, because the abuser is "sheltered in place" with them. The psalmist says (Psalm 23:5a NSRV) *"You prepare a table before me in the presence of my enemies."* Since God is the host, God's protection and care are there. Pray for that protection and that God changes the heart of the abuser. The Lord will give them the strength and courage to hold on and not despair. Know too, that God gives us discerning wisdom. If you need to seek shelter elsewhere to protect you and your family, do so.

Now, think about the young people who after putting in at least thirteen years of hard work, or four to five years of strenuous studies and are being deprived of walking across that graduation stage to receive their well-earned high school diploma or their college diploma. May they find peace and comfort in the words (Psalm 23:5b NSRV) *"You anoint my head with oil. My cup runneth over."* By them reaching this milestone in their lives, this is an affirmation that God has a plan for them.

My brothers and sisters, when the walls of stay at home, shelter in place, self-quarantine, self-isolation, the kids being out of school, "I may lose or have lost my job," the social distancing, not being able to assemble to worship and fellowship [and I do miss being with you]…when anxiety or boredom seem too much for us to handle, may these words of the psalmist give you the peace and assurance that... *(PSALM 23:6 NSRV)"* <u>*Surely*</u> *goodness and mercy shall follow me all the days of my life, and I shall dwell in the house of the Lord forever."*

As I stated earlier, we can recite the 23rd Psalm by rote, mechanically, almost like robots. But now, when we read, recite, or pray the 23rd Psalm, let us feel and believe with all our heart, mind, and soul, the words of this Psalm.

My brothers and sisters, we have a shepherd who will guide us. We have Emmanuel-God with us. We have the Holy Spirit who will comfort us. Do not lose heart. Know that this too will pass. My prayer is that today and in days to come, when you reflect and meditate on this psalm, pray this psalm, you will know and truly believe that "The Lord is indeed your Shepherd", and it is the Lord who will see all of you through.

Let us pray: *Dear God, [We are thankful that] you are our good Shepherd and we can trust you with our lives. Thank you for your leadership and Sovereignty. Thank you for your guidance and care in all our days. Thank you that you restore our souls, give us peace, and bring us hope in all our tomorrows. Thank you for your protection and strength that surrounds us like a shield. Thank you that we never have to fear. Thank you for your goodness and love that follows us, chases us, even when we are unaware. [We are thankful] that you are trustworthy and able, that you are our refuge and hope.* www.crosswalk.com/devotionals/your-daily. In You alone are rest and peace. I praise you for the assurance that I will dwell with you forever. In Jesus' Name, AMEN

YES, THERE IS!

Jeremiah 8:22

Jeremiah was a prophet who served as God's spokesperson to the people of Judah for over 40 years. The problem was that when he spoke, no one listened. The people were bent on doing things, on living their lives the way they wanted to, rejecting the directives from God. Jeremiah constantly and passionately tried to tell them "what thus saith the Lord!" He tried so hard to get the people to repent, to turn from their wicked ways, and to return to God. But again, they were set in their evil ways.

Because of this, Jeremiah stressed over the impending doom that would befall Judah. This is why he became known as the "weeping prophet." As an obedient spokesperson of the Most High, Jeremiah agonized over the messages he was told to deliver to the people. He agonized because the people refused to listen to and respond to the truth. They continued to reject his warnings from God.

Now even though the people were being hard-hearted and stiff-necked, Jeremiah was still pleading to God to save his people. In Jeremiah 8:22a NIV, he asked a rhetorical question, *"Is there no balm in Gilead?"* Balm was a resin and ointment that came from the balsam tree and was used as incense and as an ointment for healing wounds. It was a highly valued commodity and exported to other parts of the world.

Now, there was an obvious answer to the question *"Is there a balm in Gilead?"* Jeremiah knew that balm was plentiful in Gilead, but he was asking the question to make a point. Just as the balm could bring about physical healing, Jeremiah was telling the people there is a balm that can bring about spiritual healing. That balm was God. However, the people were still rejecting that which could heal their sin-sick souls. God could heal their deep spiritual wounds, but God was not going to force His healing on them. That is because God does give us free will.

When we look at what is going on today with COVID-19, we know that we need physical healing. There are still many falling ill with the virus, and still, many who are dying. But, as much as physical healing is needed, there is also a very great need for spiritual healing. 2nd Chronicle 7:14 NIV comes to mind. *"If my people who are called by my name, will humble themselves, and pray, and seek my face, turn from their wicked ways, then will I hear from heaven, and will forgive them, and heal their land."*

As a nation, we have fallen away from our Christian-Judeo roots. We, as a nation seem to have forgotten the two greatest commandments which the Lord gave. (Matthew 22:37 NIV) *"...Love the Lord your God with all your heart, your soul, and mind,"),* and to *"....love your neighbor as yourself."* (vs. 39) We, as a nation, must put back into the mainstream of life the authentic tenets and values of true Christianity. One of our members posted a clip by Roland Martin, in which he was calling televangelist and Trump spiritual advisor Paula White "on the carpet." He was talking about how she praises a man who calls himself a Christian, but whose acts are very unchristian. He referred to him as having cheap grace, meaning asking for forgiveness (even though 45 sees no need to ask for forgiveness), and then going out and doing the same thing again. There's a truthful cliché that says, "as the head goes, so does the body." We will not talk about the explosion of organizations like white supremacist groups and the Klan, or the rise in mass violence in our nation, or even the way he has handled the health crises.

As we continue to deal with COVID-19, as believers in the one who died for our sins, know that there is a balm in Gilead. That balm, my brothers and sisters, is our Lord and Savior Jesus Christ. Our enslaved ancestors put it this way as a spiritual:

Refrain:

> There is a balm in Gilead, to make the wounded whole
> *(that Jesus will give us physical healing, even from the Coronavirus)*

There is a balm in Gilead to heal the sin-sick soul *(that Jesus will give us spiritual healing, that our sins will be forgiven so we can be in right relationship with God)*

As we continue to shelter in place, stay at home, follow the directives of the health experts, our governor, and the common-sense God has given us, let us stay wise, safe, healthy, prayed up, trusting in the Lord. (2nd Tim 1:7 NIV) *"God did not give us a spirit of timidity, but of power, love, and self-discipline"* Remember my brothers and sisters, there is a balm in Gilead, and that balm is our Lord and Savior Jesus Christ.

Let us pray: Lord God, I thank you for the physical healing and the spiritual healing that can come when I put my faith and trust in You through Your son, Jesus Christ. Amen

SHELTERED IN PLACE

Psalm 91:1-3, 14-16

On March 19th, the season of Spring officially began. With spring comes much rain, and this past April, we had plenty of it, especially toward the end of the month. Despite the "shelter in place" directive, if you happened to be out and about, chances are you used an umbrella to protect yourself from the rain. Personally, I do not like using umbrellas because they can be cumbersome, and I usually end up leaving them somewhere.

When we read Psalm 91, we learn that this Psalm is about God's protection, God's umbrella if you will. It reveals a wonderful place of shelter, protection, and security. Persons of all ages, from the time of the Psalmist David to the present day have been blessed by this Psalm, for it assures us of God's protection amid danger. Understand that God does not promise us a life free from danger, but that God will be with us as we go THROUGH the danger. There is that word again, "through." I may have to walk "(Psalm 23:4a KJV) …THROUGH the valley of the shadow of death, but I will fear no evil, for Thou art with me."

I'd like us to take a look at the beginning and the end of this 91st Psalm. Stanza 91:1 (KJV) reads: "He that dwelleth in the secret place of the Most High shall abide under the shadow of the Almighty." To dwell means to inhabit, to remain, to settle in, to take up permanent residence. Those who choose to dwell in the secret place have a special relationship with God. It means a conscious decision has been made to constantly seek God's love, God's guidance, God's protection, and God's comfort. We do that by spending time with God, reading God's love letter to us, the Bible, listening to what God has to say to us through the Holy Spirit, and allowing the Holy Spirit to guide and direct us.

When we abide in the presence of God, we are promised (Psalm 91:1b KJV) *"abide in the shadow of the Almighty."* Shadows are places of protection or covering, that provide relief from the direct heat of the sun. In the summer, if we have to be outside, we usually try to find a shady spot so we are not directly in the sun. Some use an umbrella to provide that shade. The shade, not to be confused with the slang expression of "throwing shade" (the younger folk know what I'm talking about!), lessens what we feel in the intensity of the sun. It is in the shadow of the Almighty that the intensities of our trials and tribulations as lessened. The shade is our refuge, our place of safety, the place where we can find peace in God. It is in God that we can put our trust.

The 3rd stanza is so relevant for us today. It reads (Psalm 91:3 NLT) *"For He will rescue you from every trap and protect you from deadly disease."* Other translations say *deadly pestilence* (NIV), and *noisome* [repulsive, horrible, awful] *pestilence* (KJV), *deadly hazards* (MSG). Know that God protects God's people in times of plagues and diseases. Does this mean that every believer will be delivered from every snare, that is problems in life, unfair attacks from others, financial difficulties, or illnesses such as cancer, or heart problems, or COVID-19? No, it does not. Many saints have succumbed to this virus, including at least 12 bishops and many other church leaders of the Church of God in Christ.

Matthew 5:45 NIV lets us know *"...that you may be sons of your Father in Heaven; for He makes the sun to rise on the evil and the good, and sends rain on the just and the unjust."* What this does mean is that God will give us the spiritual inner strength we need to see it through to the end. My brothers and sisters! We can trust God. Even though we may not always be physically immune to the plagues, pestilence, and diseases, we are, as one writer put it, "guarded from the destructive spiritual forces as [we] dwell in the secret place of the Most High."

Psalm 91 is rich in the assurance of God's love and protection. It is filled with the goodness and power of God. It is a constant reminder that God works faithfully on behalf of those who love Him, and say and believe, that God is my refuge and fortress, my God in whom I trust. I pray that you will take the time to read, meditate, and reflect on this psalm, and receive how it speaks to you, and how it applies to your life.

Skipping down to stanzas 14-16 NLT, they read: *14 The Lord says, "I will rescue those who love me. I will protect those who trust in my name.* ¹⁵ *When they call on me, I will answer; I will be with them in trouble; I will rescue and honor them.* ¹⁶ *I will reward them with a long life and give them my salvation."* This is what God promises to those who have set their love upon God. These stanzas are specifically spoken to the people of God by God.

During the Wednesday Night Bible Study and Prayer, I read a personalized version of Psalm 91 and included it in the mailing to help us fully understand what God is saying to you and me through this Psalm. Personalizing these stanzas even more they read: *"Because you have set your love upon Me, therefore I will deliver you; I will set you on high, because you have known My name."* God will protect and keep us safe because we love God and have a sincere relationship with God.

When we are faced with danger, when we know and trust in God, we will get through our challenges. As believers and disciples of the risen Savior, we can call on the name of Jesus Christ, the most powerful name in the universe, *(Philippians 2:9b-11a NIV)* *"...the name above all names, the name upon which every knee shall bow and every tongue confess that Jesus Christ is Lord..."*

Stanzas 15-16 NIV read *¹⁵You shall call upon Me, and I will answer you; I will be with you in trouble; I will deliver you and honor you.* ¹⁶ *With long life I will satisfy you, and show you My salvation."* These are the blessings God extends to those who genuinely know and love Him. Notice how many times the pronoun "you" is used. We have the blessing of God's presence-I will be with **you** in trouble. We have the blessing of God's protection-I will deliver **you**. We have the blessing of God's promotion-I will honor **you**. We have the blessing of God's prosperity- I will satisfy **you** with long life. And we have the blessing of God's preservation-I will show **you** my salvation. When we call on God's name, God will answer us- you and me. When the enemy attacks, God will be there on our side with all His forces. Stanza 11 NIV reads *"For He will command His angels concerning you to guard you in all your ways."* God will dispatch a band of angels, seen and unseen, to protect us. When we call on God's name, God will never leave us nor forsake us.

We know that many are suffering from the loss of loved ones, some are ill, and unfortunately, some may still become ill. I praise God that to my knowledge, no members of our McMichael family or family members have been affected. When all this comes to an end, when the virus is no longer among us, when we able to return to some resemblance of normality, we will be able to look back on these days and know it was God who brought us through. We will praise God even more with praises of thanksgiving!

My brothers and sisters, let us go forth as those who dwell in the shelter of the Most High, knowing that we will find rest in the shadow of Almighty God. This is where we must "shelter in place."

Let us pray: God of love and protection, I praise and thank you for the assurance of knowing that when I am faced with the challenges of life, you are there to provide shelter for my soul, and that you will see me through. In the name of the Father, the Son, and the Holy Spirit I pray, Amen.

ARE WE THERE YET?

Isaiah 40:29

Several years ago, the rapper turned actor Ice Cube and actress Nia Long starred in a movie entitled "Are We There Yet." The movie was about a man, trying to earn brownie points with his girlfriend. He agreed to drive her rambunctious, high-spirited and lively son and daughter cross country to join their mother, who had received an unexpected work assignment. There were many adventures and misadventures.

If you've taken a road trip with children, and even adults, especially if it's a long trip, I'm sure you've heard the question, "Are we there yet?" Even though it is not written in Exodus, with my spiritual imagination, I can hear the Hebrew children asking Moses, "are we there yet?"

Life is full of challenges. If we had things our way, we would go from points A to E, bypassing B-C-and D. But that's not how life works. Know that it is not always about the destination itself, but what we learn along the way. For that which we learn along the way prepares for our destination.

When my son was 7, I had just gotten a new car (1978 powder blue Trans Am Firebird, complete with powder blue alloy rims and 8-track. As the young folk say, it was "sweet!".) I decided to put it on the road. My son, my 11-year-old sister, and I set out to go spend our Spring break with my aunt in Jackson, Tennessee. That was our destination. But on the way down, we stopped at Mammoth Cave in Kentucky. We also stopped in Huntsville, Alabama to go to the US Space and Rocket Center, and Oakwood College where my brother was in school. We finally arrived at our destination, which was Jackson, TN. Yes, it was a long trip, but the stops along the way made it fun, educational, and it was not boring. Despite this, yes, I did hear several times "Are we there yet?" but it was ok!

Today, we are on a double journey. COVID-19 has us on a journey of uncertainty, a journey of health challenges and death of loved ones, a journey of fear. Yes, the state is beginning to open, but we must continue to remain diligent and follow the directives of wearing masks in public, washing our hands, social distancing, and limiting the number of people gathered.

And then we are on a journey of dealing with the unjust treatment and deaths of black men and women at the hands of rogue police officers, and white vigilantes. These events have sparked national protests and riots throughout this nation. We have a person in the White House whose whole racist, insensitive, demeanor fuels what is happening in our country today. We cannot help but ask "Are we there yet?" Truthfully, this is a rhetorical question because we already know the answer.

When we read Isaiah 40, we learn that rather than warning the people of God's judgment for their disobedience, Isaiah is writing to encourage and comfort the people. After years of being in exile, he is letting the people know that God will reunite Israel and Judah and restore them to their former glory. Nonetheless, the people have grown tired, and have grown weary.

Like us today, we are tired and weary of this virus which has changed our whole way of living. It has changed the way we shop, the way we socialize with another, and most of all, for us and countless others, the way we worship. We are also tired and weary of the systemic racism that remains so rampant in this country, that allows white supremacist groups and racist individuals to "come out of the closet." and allows our people to be slaughtered. We remember our African Methodist Episcopal brothers and sisters that were gunned down in their church by white supremacist Dylan Roof during a Bible Study.

From the time our ancestors survived the middle passage and were enslaved, to the Civil War, to Reconstruction, to Jim Crow laws, to the Civil Rights Movement to "Black Lives Matter," "Hands Up-Don't Shoot," and "I Can't Breathe," this country's true colors have come forth. And then we are tired of the violence within our own black communities, the drug culture, the black-on-black crimes that snuff out the lives of our young black men and women. We as a people are tired, weary, worn, and sad.

But just as Isaiah had a word from the Lord for the Israelites, Isaiah also has a word for us from the Lord. In Isaiah 40:28 NIV the questions are asked, *"Do you not know? Have you not heard?"* To put it in modern terms, "Did you not get the memo?" *The Lord is the everlasting God, the creator of the ends of the earth. He will not grow tired or weary, and his understanding no one can fathom."* Even the strongest people, super athletes get tired, but God's power and strength never diminish. The good news is that God's strength is the source of our strength. God is omnipotent-all powerful, omniscience-all knowing, and omnipresent-everywhere. God is very much aware of what we are going through. When you feel like your situations, your circumstances, your illness, your financial strain, your family conflicts, your job situation, and just being sick and tired of what is going on around you, remember that you can call on the Lord to renew your strength. My brothers and sisters, (Isaiah 40:29 NIV) *"He gives strength to the weary and increases the power of the weak."* These are God's words of comfort and God's words of promise.

How do we access that strength and power? Isaiah 40:31 NIV tells us how. *"But…those who hope in the Lord will renew their strength.";* (MSG)*"But those who wait upon God get fresh strength";* (KJV) *But they that wait upon the Lord shall renew their strength;"* Waiting upon the Lord means we are assured of renewed strength. It means when we feel like giving up, when we are ready to faint away, when we're ready to throw in the towel, not only does God give us strength, but God also increases the strength that we do have. It is like getting that second, third, and fourth wind for the journey. To wait on God is not about marking time, asking the question "are we there yet?" It means we are trusting God and living with great expectation, knowing that God is working on our behalf.

When we wait on the Lord, what results can we expect? The second part of vs. 31 lets us know what happens when our strength is renewed. We will (Isaiah 40:31b NIV)*"soar on wings like eagles…"* Isaiah used the analogy of the eagle because even in Biblical times, the eagle was known for its energy, stamina, and speed. This majestic bird was seen as a symbol of strength and power. When an eagle is flying, it will flap its wings until it catches the wind, which then allows it to just soar. That is the way it is with us. When we place our hope, when we wait on the Lord, when we trust in the Lord, the Lord will renew our strength and be the "wind beneath our wings." We are then able to keep on keeping on.

And then, when we are on the ground, Isaiah lets us know we will be able to (vs. 31b) *"run and not grow weary"*, and we will *"walk and not faint"*. Whatever it is we need, whether we need the strength to soar, to be able to rise above our problems, to run and meet tour problems head-on, or to walk, to be able to bring resolution and calmness, God will give us exactly what we need at the right time.

Going back to the original question, "Are we there yet?" I think we can honestly say no, we are not there yet. But as we journey to our immediate destination which is the end of COVID-19, and the end of injustice to us as a people, which will probably be a longer journey, we learn that when we put our trust and faith in God, that we will be strengthened by the strength of the Lord. We will be able to soar on wings like eagles, we will run, and not get weary, walk, and faint not. God will give us the strength to see our journeys through to the end. And then when the question is asked "Are we there yet?", we'll be able to say, "because of God's help and strength, we are there!"

Let us pray: Eternal God, because of who you are, I know that when I wait on You, my strength to face life's situations will be renewed. Thank you, Lord. In Your name I pray, Amen.

REFUGE AT THE LORD'S TABLE

Psalm 23:5

Under normal circumstances, that is without Covid-19, the summer would have been a time of big family get-togethers, picnics, dinners, and reunions. You get to see how the family has increased and remember those who are no longer with us. There would be great tables set with plenty of food, prepared with a lot of tender loving care. Here in south Louisiana, you know there would be plenty of gumbo, red beans and rice, fried catfish, crawfish, crabs, jambalaya, fried chicken, cornbread, okra and tomato stew, greens, mac-n-cheese, bread pudding with real rum sauce, and refreshing ice tea. There is a sense of security that goes along with most family gatherings because you know that regardless of what happens, your family is there, and will be there for you. These gatherings become a source of refuge and strength for us. This morning, I would like to share with you a source of refuge and strength from another table, which brings me to our sermon focus, **REFUGE AT THE LORD'S TABLE.**

Refuge can be defined as protection from danger, a shelter, or a haven during challenging and difficult times. Refuge is what we seek when we are in what seems like an unbearable situation. Refuge, shelter, and safety are what we seek when there is a hurricane, tornado, or flood, or in the case of our brothers and sisters on the West Coast, uncontrolled fires.

Refuge can be as simple as a child running to Grandma or Grandpa because they have been chastised by mom or dad. Or, it can be as serious and life-threatening as a mother and her children slipping away in the middle of the night to escape the tyranny of a physically, mentally, and/or emotionally abusive spouse or companion.

1st Samuel 21 tells us how David was forced to escape the wrath of Saul. The king and David had returned from a victorious battle, and as they entered the city, the ladies began that infamous chant (1st Samuel 18:7 NIV) *"Saul has slain his thousands, and David his ten thousand."* Already feeling insecure because of all the attention David was receiving, especially from the ladies, Saul became filled with envy, jealousy, and hate. He reacted by trying to destroy and kill David. Out of fear, and a strong sense of self-preservation, David fled to the hills and sought refuge in a cave.

As people of God, through prayer, we continuously seek refuge from the evil and satanic forces that are ever-present in our midst. Again, refuse is what we seek when we need shelter and protection from dangers seen and unseen, and situations that seem too tough and hard for us to handle. We also seek shelter in things that make us feel good about ourselves, that we feel help to boost our sense of self-worth and importance. What are some of those things we seek as refuge?

There are those who seek refuge in material wealth and possessions, in the tangible "here today, gone tomorrow" things. We believe that the more we have, the better off we are. Now do not misunderstand what I'm saying. Being able to have is a blessing from God, and a blessing not to be taken lightly. Believe me, the Lord has been good to me, and for that I am thankful. I always look forward to being even more blessed by God. The problem comes when our whole sense of being and purpose in life is directly tied to how much we have, be it money, a big house, a fine car. When this happens, then we are seeking refuge in the wrong place.

Many seek refuge through social status and education. They tend to boast on the fact that they have reached a particular level of academic achievement and/or status in their community. These are the ones who wear their job titles and college degrees on their shoulders like a neon light. I'm talking about those whose conversations revolve around how important they are in their community or civic organization. These are the ones whom Paul told (Romans 12:3b NIV) *"Do not think of yourself more highly than you ought to think...."*

One of the most common forms of seeking refuge is through the abusive use of alcohol and drugs. These persons attempt to find their refuge, that comfort zone, by getting high, drowning themselves and their problems in Crown Royal, Jack Daniels, Wild Irish Rose, cocaine, or crack. The refuge may be there for a little while, but when they come off that high, they realize the problem is still there, staring them in the face. And because of the abuse, the problem has probably intensified.

And then there are those who seek or have sought refuge through sexual gratification. Many persons, both female and male, fall into a trap of sexual promiscuity, not because they have low moral values, but because they are seeking some form of emotional refuge, which is often mistaken for love. We all want to and need to be loved. This is the way God created us. Unfortunately, many men and women become innocently, and some not so innocently, victimized by persons whose intentions are less than honorable.

Again, what we are talking about this morning is refuge, a place of shelter and protection, a place of comfort in a time of trouble. In the 23rd Psalm, David lets us know that such a place does indeed exist. The 5th stanza NIV reads *"You prepare a table before me in the presence of my enemies; you anoint my head with oil; my cup overflows."* David is letting us know that we can find REFUGE AT THE LORD'S TABLE. Just to clarify, I am not referring to the New Testament Communion Table and the Lord's Supper that we will celebrate a little later. I am talking about the table of refuge, a place of strength and protection.

What is it the Lord has to offer us at this very special table? First of all, God welcomes us to the table with a feast, a banquet prepared just for you and me. (Stanza 5a KJV) *"Thou preparest a table before me."* God knows our specific needs and tailors each meal individually. Part of the jingle from an old Burger King commercial was "special orders don't upset us, have it your way." Well, the difference between Burger King and the Lord's table is that you do not have to place an order, because God already knows just what you need, be it healing, comfort in the loss of a loved one, peace in your home, providing tuition. Let us keep in mind now, that our wants are not always our needs. In God's infinite wisdom, God discerns our needs and makes the provision. Remember that (Philippians 4:19 NIV) *"... my God will meet all of your needs, according to His glorious riches in Christ Jesus."*

In addition to a great feast, God offers us protection. (stanza 5 KJV) *"Thou preparest a table before me...in the presence of my enemies."* Since God is the host, the presence of David's enemies is no threat to him. He is there under God's watchful eye, and God's wings of protection and care. It is sort of like being chased home by the school bully, making it to your front porch, and having your big sister or brother or one of your parents standing there with you. You know they have got your back. You are feeling safe, secure, confident, and even bold enough to stick out your tongue and start "selling wolf tickets." You know your enemy can do you no harm.

When we seek refuge at the Lord's table, we also find acceptance. (stanza 5c KJV) *"Thou anointest my head with oil."* In the days of David, it was customary and proper etiquette for the host to rub a sweet fragrant oil on the head of the guest. This was the host's way of letting the guest know that he or she was indeed welcomed into their home. With God, it matters not where you have been or even where you are now. To come to the Lord's table, you don't have to get your hair and nails done or change into your "Sunday go to meetin' clothes." You do not have to wait until you have kicked that alcohol or drug habit. God knows what is going on in your life and in your heart. And when you come to the Lord's table seeking refuge, God accepts you just the way you are. This is probably what Charlotte Elliot had in mind when she penned the words to that great hymn of the church:

Just as I am, Thou wilt receive
Wilt welcome (accepts you),
pardon (forgives you),
cleanse (help you to leave those negative elements of your life behind),
relieve (you no longer have to bear the guilt of your sins).
Because Thy promise, I believe,
O Lamb of God I come, I come.

When we seek refuge at the Lord's table, God offers us love, kindness, unconditional loving-kindness, a love with no strings attached. We do not have to go through a song and dance or jump hoops to receive God's love. All we have to do is open our hearts, our minds, and our spirits to receive God's precious gift of love.

And finally, my beloved brothers and sisters, God is generous. David wrote, (stanza 5d KJV) *"My cup runneth over."* God has so much, such an abundance to offer us. After all, (Psalm 24:1 KJV) *"The earth is the Lord's and the fullness thereof."* The God we serve is like any other loving parent.

God wants to provide those things we need and desire and is by no means stingy or selfish. As Paul told the Philippians, (4:19 KJV) *"But my God shall supply all your need according to his riches in glory by Christ Jesus."* I had a pastor who would say, "My Daddy is rich, and He loves me!"

When we seek refuge at the Lord's table, we find a feast prepared just for you and me. We find protection from our enemies. We find God's acceptance and unconditional love. And, we find God's generosity.

After we have sufficiently dined at the Lord's table, what is it we can expect when we leave? Well, you do not and won't have to leave empty-handed. We can leave, if you will, with a "doggie bag", filled with God's blessings and grace. This enables us to return and face the realities of life, knowing that God will supply all of our needs, knowing that God accepts us with all of our human imperfections, knowing that God loves us unconditionally, and knowing that God will see us through the adversities of life.

If you want to experience that refuge found at the Lord's table, prepare to receive the feast of a lifetime. And you know what else is wonderful about this table? You can always come back for second, third, fourth helpings, and more. You do not ever have to feel embarrassed about being or looking greedy or the feast offerings running out. The Lord wants us to return any time we need to and any time we want.

There may be someone on the call this morning who is saying to themselves "I definitely need to come to this table, but how do I get there?" As I stated earlier, you just come. You come just as you are. But Rev. Pat, I was not invited. I am here to tell you that you were invited over 2000 years ago when Christ died on Calvary for all of our sins. All you need is a desire to have God, God's only begotten son, our Lord and Savior Jesus Christ, and the power of the Holy Spirit to be the central guiding force in your life.

Perhaps you have not accepted Christ as your Lord and Savior, you have never feasted at the Lord's table. Come now and give your life to Christ and be saved, and experience the joy of salvation. Or maybe you have grown away from the church and you know it's time for you to come back to the Lord's table. Or maybe you are coming from another church and wish to be united with the McMichael family of believers.

Whatever the case may be, if you are out of that arch of safety and need to have a closer walk with God, in need of a place to study the Word of God, a place to be in fellowship with other believers, a place to work out your soul's salvation, won't you make yourself known. Virtually give me your hand in fellowship and give God your heart. Know, my beloved, there is REFUGE AT THE LORD'S TABLE!

Let us pray: Lord God, I thank you for the forgiveness, protection, unconditional love, and bountiful generosity You offer at Your table. Lord, let me have an even closer walk with you. In Your name I pray, Amen.

GOD'S GIFT OF REPENTANCE

Acts 2: 34-41

This has been one heck of a week for our nation. We went through the November 3rd election for the president of the United States as well as state and local elections. As I was preparing this message, the outcome of the presidential election still has not been finalized, although the writing was clearly on the wall. One reporter said the difference in the percentages is razor-thin, like in Georgia, 49.4 to 49.4 percent. That is crazy.

One thing for sure is crystal clear. The United States is a divided nation. It will be the daunting task of the next administration to bring this country back under the banner of a unified nation. But you know what, there is no need for us to fret, to be discouraged, or scared because we know who is in control. Our faith and trust are in our sovereign, omnipotent, omniscient, omnipresent almighty God. As I posted, "I prayed, I voted, I am trusting God."

We now know that our president for the next four years is President-elect Joseph Biden, with vice president-elect Kamala Harris, the first African-American woman to be elected to that office. To God be the glory. Let us keep them, the transition teams, and the entire administration to come lifted in prayer. And let us continue to pray for the current, soon-to-be ex-president, who is having an exceedingly difficult time accepting defeat.

This morning, I would like to focus on the subject of repentance, which is turning away from sin. Proverbs 28:13 NIV tells us *"Whoever conceals their sins does not prosper, but the one who confesses and renounces them finds mercy."* God desires truth in our heart, mind, and spirit, and commands that all persons everywhere repent. For us to receive God's gift of salvation which comes by grace through our faith in Jesus Christ, we must turn from our sinful ways. Even after we have received and accepted the salvation of our Lord and Savior Jesus Christ, we must continue to repent for those sins, big and small, known and unknown, that we commit on a day-to-day basis.

The book "Respectable Sins" by Jerry Bridges outlines those sins, that we may not even realize are sins, those actions which none less, are displeasing in the sight of God. They include pride, selfishness, ingratitude, ungodliness, anger, impatience, envy, jealousy, judgmentalism, a lying, cruel, and deceitful tongue.

It was Job who prayed for his seven sons and three daughters who feasted together, who ate, drank, and partied together. Job 1:5 NIV says *"When a period of feasting had run its course, Job would make arrangements for them to be purified. Early in the morning he would sacrifice a burnt offering for each of them, thinking, "Perhaps my children have sinned and cursed God in their hearts."* This was Job's regular custom."

This is a life lesson for us as parents, grandparents, and guardians. Every day, we should pray and lift our children to the Lord, to ask God to protect them, to guide them, to help them make wise decisions. No matter how old that child gets, even if he or she is 60 years old, continue to pray for them.

Repentance, my brothers and sisters, is about change, turning from that which is not of God, to doing and being that which is pleasing to God. True repentance is mainly evidenced by three characteristics. The first characteristic is intellectual, a change in the way we think. Romans 12:2 NIV reads *"Do not conform to the pattern of the world, be transformed [changed] by the renewing of your mind. Then you be able to test and approve what God's will is-God's good, pleasing, and perfect will."* Know my brothers and sisters, that even though we may avoid the most obvious worldly sins such as murder and grand larceny, we are still susceptible to those "respectable sins," such as pride, jealousy, selfishness, judgmentalism. Only when the Holy Spirit renews, re-educates, and redirects our thoughts, our minds, are we truly transformed. Allow your mind to be renewed by the power of the Holy Spirit.

And then, for true repentance to take place, there has to be an emotional change, a change in our hearts. We are familiar with David's plea in Psalm 51:10 KJV that says, *"Create in me a clean heart, and renew a right spirit within me."* Like David, we must ask God to cleanse us on the inside, to cleanse our hearts, to remove those negative feelings, those negative attitudes that we tend to harbor in our hearts. That cleansing, that change is evidenced by our actions and by what flows from our mouths. Proverbs 4:23-24 NIV tells us *"23 Above all else, guard your heart, for it is the well-spring of life. 24 Put away perversity from your mouth, keep corrupt talk from your lips."* The Message translation says it this way: *23 Keep vigilant watch over your heart; that's where life starts. 24 Don't talk out of both sides of your mouth; avoid careless banter [teasing, making fun of], white lies, and gossip [also known as "shoo-shooing"].*

Solomon is letting us know that what is in our hearts dictates how we live. We are to protect our hearts, making sure we focus and concentrate on those desires that will keep us on the path of repentance and salvation. On this spiritual journey, make sure you keep your heart fixed on the goal, which is fellowship with God through Jesus Christ, empowered by the Holy Spirit. Do not get sidetracked by the detours of life that can lead to sin. My brothers and sisters, GUARD YOUR HEART!

Finally, there is the characteristic of volition, which is a deliberate and conscious change in our actions. Luke 15:11-32 tells the story of the prodigal son. He demanded his inheritance from his father, which his father gave him. The son, who had probably never been away from his family, went to the big city, squandered his money, and ended up fighting the pigs for something to eat. During his pity party, he had an epiphany, an intuitive, insightful, and instinctual grasp of reality. In the words of Fresh Prince's Hilary Banks, he had a true "DUH!" moment. Luke 15:17-18 NIV reads, *17 "When he came to himself, he said 'How many of my father's hired men have had food to spare, and here I am starving to death. 18 I will set out and go back to my father and say to him, Father, I have sinned against heaven and you'"*

I am sure we have all had our spiritual "DUH" moments. I know I have. We know we must change the way we are living, and/or the way we are doing things, to be right with God. We have to change our actions. And if you have been (Proverbs 22:6) *"...trained as a child in the way you should go...,"* that convicting "DUH" moment will go straight to your heart.

That change can be breaking off a relationship you know you have no business being in. It can be coming to the reality that your body is the temple of God, and that you need to stop abusing and destroying it with excessive eating, drugs, and alcohol. You might need to change the way you treat your spouse or significant other, and family members, especially if there is physical, mental, or emotional abuse involved. That change might be how you treat your neighbors, your co-workers, your classmates, and even your brothers and sisters at church. But most of all, that volitional change must be that conscience decision to turn away from a life of sin, to repent by turning to God through His Son Jesus Christ.

Like the prodigal son, sometimes we must be broken before that "DUH" moment of reality hits us, and we realize that we have to turn to God with a repentant heart. In the hymn, A Broken Heart, My God My King, hymn writer Isaac Watts put it this way:

A broken heart, my God, my King, to Thee a sacrifice I bring;
The God of grace will ne'er despise, a broken heart for sacrifice.

My soul lies humbled in the dust, and owns Thy dreadful sentence just;
Look down O Lord with pitying eye, and save the soul condemned to die.

O may Thy love inspire my tongue! Salvation shall be all my song;
And all my powers shall join to bless the Lord, my strength and righteousness.

As we continue on this unknown path of Covid-19, dealing with the hope of our nation being reunited, of our congregation coming together as one, regardless of what happens, don't let anything or anyone cause you to take your eyes off of your spiritual focus, which is God's gift of repentance that leads to salvation and being in right relationship with God.

Let us pray: Lord God, please change my spiritual "DUH" moments to a focus on Your Son Jesus Christ so that I may receive your true gift of repentance and salvation. In Jesus name I pray, Amen.

SPECIAL DAYS

1st SUNDAY OF LENT

Don't Let The Devil Fool Ya!

Luke 4:1-13

When I hear the word temptations, being from the Motor City, home of Motown, my mind automatically goes to that fabulous quintet of brothers that gave us hit songs like "The Way You Do the Things You Do," "My Girl", Beauty's Only Skin Deep", "Since I Lost My Baby", and countless others. And the thing is, those old school songs sound just as good and fresh as they did when I was in junior high and high school. Come on Baby Boomers, don't act like you don't know what I'm talking about! You know back in the day you did some serious partying to those tunes!

When they went to audition at Motown, they were told by the executives to step outside and come back with a new name. The name Elgins was not working for them. After a serious conversation, somehow the concept of "forbidden" came up, which led to the word temptation. Thus, one of the world's greatest male singing groups was on its way to fame and fortune.

Now I know many of you are wondering what do the Temptations have to do with this morning's message. Let us cross that bridge and look at the scripture that was read, and even back up to the last two verses of chapter 3. Jesus had been baptized by his cousin John (the Baptist). Verses 16-17 NKJV tell us *"16 As soon as Jesus was baptized, he came up immediately from the water; and behold, the heavens were opened to Him, and He saw the Spirit of God descending like a dove and alighting upon Him. 17 And suddenly a voice came from heaven, saying, "This is my beloved Son in whom I am well pleased."* Chapter 4 begins with *"Then Jesus was led up by the Spirit into the wilderness to be tempted by the devil."* And tempted He was.

Understand my brothers and sisters, the devil is not symbolic, but a real spiritual being and his temptations are real. He is constantly coming against those who strive to follow and obey God. The devil tries to do the same thing to us he was trying to do to Jesus. He is trying to derail you and me from God's plan and purpose for our lives! Satan knew that the incarnate Jesus Christ came to save us from our sins, to teach how to love one another, and to give us life, so we could have life more abundantly.

This time in the wilderness was Jesus' period of transition, of preparing for his earthly ministry. Matt. 4:2 lets us know that after forty days and forty nights of fasting and praying, he was hungry, tired, weak, and in a very vulnerable state. This is when the devil came to him. Remember, Jesus was both divine and human, and it was the human side that satan was going after. However, also knowing the divine power Jesus had, satan tried to get Jesus to turn stones into bread, tried to get him to test God by throwing himself from the highest point of the temple, and tried to entice him with power and possession by offering him the kingdoms of the world. Look at the progression of satan's temptations: hunger, pride, and power and possession.

Do not, my brothers and sisters be fooled. Satan is as real today as he was over 2000 years ago. Just as he came to Jesus, he comes to us in the same way. And just know, it is not a matter of if he attacks, but when he attacks. Satan will attack us at our points of weakness, like when we are physically, emotionally, mentally, or spiritually stressed. Satan will attack us when we have problems or situations that are going wrong. He presents a way out which looks good, a way out of your troubles and problems, but you know is not right, nor is it pleasing to God.

When you and your spouse or significant other are having problems, the devil will tempt you with that handsome gentleman or beautiful young lady that has been trying to get your attention. When you have a test coming up and you feel ill-prepared, the devil will tempt you to cheat. And when you've prayed for something, and it seems God is not hearing you, the devil will whisper in your ear that God doesn't care, and tempt you to do things your own way.

Satan will also attack when we are doing well, when we are riding on a crest of popularity, when we are receiving accolades for a job well done, or when we are achieving great success. This is where pride can enter our spirits, and we know that (Proverbs 16:18 NIV) *"pride goes before destruction."*

Remember, satan is a fallen angel who once resided in heaven. He was cast out of heaven because he became jealous of God and felt he should be exalted above God rather than serve Him. Rather than accept that he was not greater than God, he accepted being cast from heaven so he could put his plan to work…that was and is to destroy the work of God.

Let us take a closer look at how satan tempted Jesus. He said to Jesus (Luke 4:3 NKJV) *"If* (trying to plant a seed of doubt) *you are the Son of God, command this stone to become bread."* That is the way Satan works. He uses his adversaries to create doubt and will have you second-guessing yourself. Know who you are and whose you are! Satan knew Jesus had the divine power to change the stones, but Jesus put aside his unlimited use of divine power to fully experience being human. He would not use his divine power to satisfy his natural hunger, the same type of physical hunger we experience when we fast.

For those of you who are fasting during this Lenten season, giving up a particular food item/items, or cutting back on surfing the internet or watching particular TV shows, tell the attacker as Jesus told him, (Matthew 4:4 NKJV) *"Man shall not live by bread alone, but by every word that proceeds from the mouth of God*. That is why daily reading and meditating on God's word and praying are vital to fasting. When we are going through trials and tribulations, we can take comfort in knowing that Jesus knows and understands what we are going through. If Jesus were with us today in the flesh, he would probably tell us, "been there, done that, wrote the book!"

Next, satan took Jesus to the Holy City, set Him on the highest point of the temple, and told Him (Luke 4:9b NIV) *"If* (again trying to plant a seed of doubt), *you are the Son of God, …throw yourself down from here"* This is where satan really tried to be slick. He is trying to appeal to Jesus with what he perceives as an emotional need for security. Satan knew the Word of God and tried to use it. He quoted Psalm 91:11-12 NIV which reads *11"For he will command his angels concerning you to guard you in all your ways; they will lift you up in their hands, so that you will not strike your foot against a stone."* In other words, satan was telling Jesus that if you jump off the top of this temple, you will not get hurt. He intentionally misinterpreted and misused the word of God to suit his personal agenda.

Now, if satan knew, and knows the Word of God, it behooves us to know it just as well, and even more so. Many believers have been thrown off track because of the way God's Word has been twisted and misinterpreted. Verses taken out of context can be presented in a way that is attractive and provides convincing reasons why you should do something you know is wrong. And it is accepted because the hearer does not know the Word of God for himself or herself. Again, that is why it is important, imperative to read, study, and know God's word. Don't, my brothers and sisters, let the devil fool ya!

As a church body, during this Lenten season and beyond, it is my sincere prayer that we be intentional about reading and studying God's Word. I have no problem whatsoever if you have your Bibles open while I am preaching to make sure I am doing my best in presenting myself to God as one (2ⁿᵈ Timothy 2:15 NKJV) *"... approved to God, a worker who does not need to be ashamed, rightly dividing the Word of Truth."* I want us individually and collectively to get to the point where we enjoy reading God's Word so much, that it's hard to put down.

In the worship guide, I have included a Lenten Bible Reading Plan that will take us through the four Gospels, from the birth of Christ to the Resurrection. During the Advent season, many of us read through the gospel according to St. Luke. It will not hurt to read it again. God may give you new and additional insight. Having the Word of God in our heart, mind, and spirit gives us strength to face whatever adversity comes our way.

Finally, satan now pulls out all the stops. He takes Jesus to a very high mountain and shows him all the kingdoms of the world. Matthew 4: 9 NKJV says *"And he said to Him, "All these things I will give You if* (not a seed of doubt this time, but stating a condition) *you fall down and worship me."* First of all, the devil was being a "perceived legend in his mind," because the kingdoms of the world were not his to give. They belong to God. He was trying to appeal to a human need for power and position.

Today, the devil offers us the world by trying to entice us with materialism, popularity, prestige, and power. In and of themselves, these are not bad, because they can very well be blessings from God. The problem comes when we place these things above God, and they become our idols.

In my spiritual imagination, I think satan thought he had worn Jesus down and Jesus was ready to give in. He is probably rubbing his hands together, getting ready to "go in for the kill." However!!! Jesus was strengthened from within. He boldly declared (Matthew 4:10 *NKJV*) "… *Away with you Satan! For it is written, you shall worship the Lord your God, and Him only will you serve.*" KJV says "*Get thee hence!*"; The NIV says "*Away from me Satan!*"; TLB-'*Get out of here Satan;* MSG- "*Beat it Satan!*

Jesus backed his rebuke with a third quotation from Deuteronomy: (Matthew 4:10) '*You shall worship the* LORD *your God, and Him only you shall serve.*' Satan knows he's lost this round! Luke ends Jesus' wilderness experience with Luke 4:13 NIV "*Now when the devil had ended every temptation, he departed from Him until an opportune time.*" In other words, in the words of the Terminator, "I'll be back!" When the devil is trying to entice us in any way, and trust me, he will, like Jesus, boldly declare "Satan, beat it! Get away from me." Or as the PAB version (that's me) blatantly declares, "Satan, go back to hell!"

We know that Lent is the period in which we especially identify with Christ's wilderness experience. It is a period of personal sacrifice, of giving up or cutting back on something we like to eat or enjoy, as an act of penitence. Again, this Lenten season, I would like us to think in terms of doing something, which is to commit to reading our Bibles every day. Even if you do not follow the Lenten Reading Plan in the worship guide, read something from the Bible. And as you read, jot down thoughts and insights that the Holy Spirit gives you, and questions you may have.

And before you read, pray for the Lord to open your mind, heart, and spirit to receive the message God gives you. You and I may read the same passage of scripture and the Holy Spirit will give us different insights. When those different insights are shared, we all can receive new and additional insight into the spirit of God.

As we continue our Lenten journey, let us do so with a prayerful commitment to read and study the Word of God so that, just as Jesus did, we too will be able to stand strong and firm, and be strengthened against the attacks and wiles of the devil and his adversaries. My brothers and sisters! Don't let the devil fool ya!

Reverend Patricia A. Turner-Brown

Let us pray: Lord God, as I travel my spiritual journey, when faced with temptations, strengthen me to be able to resist the wiles of the devil. Let me too be able to declare "Satan, beat it! Get away from me." In Jesus name I pray, Amen

PALM SUNDAY

Oh, What A Week!

Matthew 21:1-11

With all that is going on with the COVID-19 coronavirus…the lockdowns, stay at home, shelter in place, social distancing, quarantines, curfew mandates …businesses being closed, workers being classified as essential or non-essential, many losing their jobs…in all of this, know that God is still with us. God has, and for some folk, is still getting our attention. Despite everything, God is letting us know that we are not forgotten nor abandoned. Even amid our doubts, our struggles, our fears, our uncertainties, know that God is with us. We can stand on the promise that God will never leave us nor forsake us.

God is using this time of forced slowdown, this involuntary shutdown to invite us into a deeper relationship with Him. Those things and events that would often hinder us from spending time with God, such as sporting events, hanging out at the malls and shopping, weekend jaunts to the local "watering holes", have been eliminated. Even physically spending time with family and friends, has been seriously curtailed. This time of upheaval, my brothers and sisters, is our opportunity to draw closer to God. This is the time to daily focus on prayer and to read and reflect on the Word of God.

Today is recognized as Palm Sunday, the day that Christ made His triumphal entry into Jerusalem. Jews had come from all over the Roman empire to Jerusalem in preparation for the Passover celebration, many coming to see Jesus. Some came because they knew of Jesus' miraculous healings, of his feeding of the 5000, of his forgiveness, of his love. Many had experienced his ministry firsthand. Wherever Jesus went He drew a crowd. His entry into Jerusalem is one of the few places where the Gospel writers record that the glory and majesty of Jesus were recognized on earth. Jesus even boldly declared himself as King, and the crowd gladly joined him.

Those in the crowd were waving palms, which were symbols of victory and triumph. This is akin to us being at a political rally and waving an American flag, or a sporting event waving the foam finger. The crowd was shouting "Hosanna to the Son of David", "Blessed is He who comes in the name of the Lord". "Hosanna in the highest." Hosana is essentially a plea for salvation, "save us", and those in the crowd truly saw Jesus as their Savior.

Today is also recognized as Passion Sunday, the beginning of Holy Week, and oh what a week it was! One commentator describes Passion Sunday as "the beginning of the end because the events of the week led to Christ's Crucifixion five days later." Monday is the day Jesus went to the Jerusalem temple and threw a temper tantrum, a holy rage. Matthew 21:12-13 NIV reads *12 Then Jesus went into the temple of God and drove out all those who bought and sold in the temple, and overturned the tables of the money-changers and the seats of those who sold doves. 13 And He said to them, "It is written, 'My house shall be called a house of prayer,' but you have made it a 'den of thieves.'"*

On Tuesday, Jesus returned to the temple and was confronted by the religious leaders who were upset with him because he had disrupted their extra source of income. Knowing that they were plotting, trying to find an excuse to arrest and kill him, Jesus ended up calling them a bunch of hypocrites and vipers.

It is believed that after two physically and emotionally challenging and exhausting days, Jesus took Wednesday to relax and prepare for the Passover celebration on Thursday. Wednesday, also known as Spy Wednesday is the day Judas Iscariot made his deal with the Sanhedrin Council to betray Jesus and have Jesus arrested. This was done for thirty pieces of silver, which in today's market would be worth between $185-$216.

This brings us to what we know as Maundy Thursday. It was on this day that Jesus agonized in the Garden of Gethsemane. Matthew 26:42b

NIV tells us he prayed . *"My Father, if it is possible, may this cup be taken from me. Yet not as I will, but as you will."* He and his disciples then gathered in the Upper Room to celebrate the Passover together. It was at this table, that Jesus established what we now know as Communion or the Lord's Supper.

Today, on Palm Sunday, we also celebrate communion, receiving the elements of bread and wine. Yes, it will be quite different. I pray that you take today's communion service just as seriously as you would if you were kneeling at the altar at McMichael. The elements of the Lord's Supper will be what you have…crackers, bread, water, juice. But please know, when they are consecrated, these elements become the symbols of the body and blood of Christ. Christ used the bread and wine to represent his body and blood. The Lord's Supper was instituted by Christ to strengthen our faith.

At this time in our lives, during this pandemic, our faith needs to be strengthened each day. We are all facing one challenge or another. Each day we are inundated with numbers, the number of persons who have contracted the virus, and the number of persons who have succumbed to this illness. I am sure every single one of us knows someone who has contracted the virus or has even passed away because of the virus. As of yesterday, Tangipahoa Parish reported 55 cases and one death.

My brothers and sisters, we have got to stay prayed up. And as a quick aside, I want to thank those who participated in the Wednesday Night Prayer. There were prays offered by members of the McMichael family, both clergy and the laity for our first responders, government officials, health care workers, students, seniors, and for the elimination of the virus. My McMichael family, we are going to pray our way through this pandemic. We are going to uphold one another in prayer. We are going to check on one another. We are going to be the body of believers Christ has called us to be.

As we celebrate Palm Sunday, remember Christ came as the King of kings, and Lord of lords. He came to show us how to love one another, how to forgive one another. He came to show us how to serve one another. He came that we might have life and have it more abundantly.

And as we share in the Lord's Supper, remember that Christ gave his body to be broken, and he poured out his blood for our transgressions. He had the power to come down off the cross, but he did not. He died for our sins. As we enter Holy Week, let us be mindful of Christ's final week on earth, and oh what a week it was. Know that this week leads to the reason for our existence as a Body of Believers, that is the glorious Resurrection of our Lord and Savior, Jesus the Christ.

Let us pray: Loving God, may I always be in the Palm Sunday crowd that shouts "Hosana in the Highest", Blessed is He who comes in the name of the Lord!" In the name of Jesus the Christ I pray, Amen.

GOOD FRIDAY
Good News For Today

Luke 23:39-43

In today's world, the news media offers very little good news. We are daily, hourly inundated with news and updates regarding the coronavirus. How many have been affected, how many have died. It is good, and necessary to remain informed, but do not let it consume your mind and spirit. It will create in your spirit a strong sense of gloom and doom.

If we continuously allow ourselves to be fed by the negative news from the news media, we miss the good news that that is all around us. Many individuals have recovered from the virus. Tyler Perry paid for the groceries of senior citizens who shopped at Atlanta's Winn-Dixie and Kroger's. Families are spending more time together and being creative in celebrating special occasions, such as birthdays.

Going back to the scripture that was read, I would like to lift Luke 23:43 NIV, which reads *"Jesus answered him, "Truly I tell you, today you will be with me in paradise.""* For a few moments, let us focus on the thought **GOOD NEWS FOR TODAY"**

Go with me if you will, back in history, over 2000 years ago. Close your eyes and go with me to Golgotha, the Place of the Skull, to Calvary. There he is, Jesus the Christ, the Messiah, the beloved Son of God, our Lord and Savior, being crucified. There he is, hanging on the cross, the most humiliating form of torture and execution of that day. It was so humiliating, that crucifixions were reserved only for slaves and criminals. To the Jews, this was the most offensive form of death.

Keep in mind now, that it was the elite and educated Sanhedrin Council-the high priest, Pharisees and Sadducees, the scribes and elders that turned Jesus over to the Roman government and insisted that he be executed this way. Even when Pilate gave them the opportunity to recant on what he knew were trumped up charges, and said (John 19:14b-15 NIV) *"Here is your King" Pilate said to the Jews. ¹⁵ But they shouted, "Take him away...Crucify him...We have no king but Caesar!" and* (Luke 23:18b NIV) *"... Away with this man. Release Barabbas to us"* Finally, against his own conscience and the advice of his wife, Pilate handed Jesus over to them to be crucified. After Jesus was spat on, beat with a whip that had sharp stone shards that tore into his flesh, and a crown created with one-inch pointed thorns pressed on and into his head, he was forced to carry his own cross.

Let us look at the cross itself. I am sure the skilled unionized Roman carpenters did not go to Home Depot or Lowes and purchase smooth marine board planks. No! Using my spiritual imagination, I believe some "ol' boys" found two tree trunks that were about the size they needed for the task. They then sawed and hacked until they were able to form the two pieces of wood into the shape of a cross, splinters and all. As the hymn writer George Bennard described, it was on this "old, rugged cross" that our Savior was crucified.

To add insult to injury, after the soldiers nailed our Lord to that cross, they raised him between two common criminals, two thieves. There they were, this mismatched trio, experiencing the same type of humiliating, tortuous, and painful death.

As life was slowly seeping from their bodies, the crowd that gathered to watch were shouting mocking insults at Christ. (Matthew 27:40 NIV) *"You who are going to destroy the temple and build it back in three days, save yourself. "Come down from the cross if you are the Son of God."* Even the chief priests, the scribes, and the elders were mocking Jesus. *(vs. 42) "He saved others, but can't save himself." (vs. 43) "... He trusts in God. Let God rescue him now, if he wants him..."* Notice the sarcasm.

Luke 23:39 NIV tells us that one of the thieves joined the crowd in mocking Jesus. *"...Aren't you the Christ? Save yourself and us!"* I think the thief's reason for insulting Jesus was different from the crowd. For this thief, it was about self-preservation. He probably knew just enough about

Jesus to know that He had performed many lifesaving miracles. So why not now? I sure he was probably thinking, "If you are who you claim to be, then get yourself, and us out of here!"

The second thief could not believe what he heard coming from the lips of the other thief. He knew the two of them deserved to be on that hill. He knew they were guilty of their accused crimes. This thief, however, knew just enough about Jesus to know Jesus did not deserve the punishment he was receiving. He also knew enough about Jesus to know that if he repented, he could, and would be forgiven. He knew that if he asked the Savior, he would be pardoned of his sins.

With a tremendous sense of humility, and an even greater sense of faith and hope in what seemed to be a hopeless situation, the second thief turned his head to the Savior and said, (Luke 23:42 NIV) *"...Jesus, remember me when you come into your kingdom."* Now in the midst of his own physical pain, suffering, and misery, and knowing that he was taking on the sins of all humanity, Jesus had some good news for the thief. Jesus answered him saying, (vs. 43) *"I tell you the truth, today, you will be with me in paradise."*

My brothers and sisters! Know that the response of Christ to the thief over 2000 years ago has the same power and relevance for us today as it did then. Today! That is a powerful word. Not tomorrow, after you have cleaned up your act and gotten your life together. Not after you have kicked that substance abuse habit, or after you have been punished by society. Not after you have broken your marriage vows. Not even after you have been baptized or read through the Bible ten times and have it memorized from Genesis to Revelation. Not even after you have been to church every night this week and twice on Sunday.

The good news is Jesus' pardoning grace, mercy and forgiveness is available for us today, right here and right now! What then, someone might be asking, must I do to receive the pardoning grace of Jesus? Like the dying thief, we too must come to Christ with a repentant heart and contrite spirit, accepting through faith in Jesus Christ, that our sins will be forgiven. We must also purpose in our hearts to turn away from, that is to earnestly repent of that which separates us from God, and turn, with intentionality to that which will lead us to full and spiritually rich lives in Jesus Christ.

We are now just about at the end of our Lenten journey. We look forward with great anticipation to Resurrection Sunday to celebrate our risen Lord and Savior. My prayer is that individually and collectively as a church family, our Lenten journey has been a period of spiritual growth, and that all of us now have an even closer walk with God.

My beloved brothers and sister in Christ, like the dying thief on Calvary's hill, let us in faith receive our full pardon from Jesus Christ, and go forth as redeemed and forgiven children of God and disciples of Jesus Christ.

Let us pray: Lord Jesus, thank you for dying for my sins. Because of your crucifixion I no longer have to carry the burden of my sins. For that, I offer you my heart with praise and thanksgiving. In the precious name of my crucified, soon to be Resurrected Savior Jesus the Christ, Amen.

RESURRECTION DAY

The Hope And Glory
Of The Resurrection

Matthew 28:1-10

We are living in a strange and bizarre time, a time in history, where America, and nations around the world, have been shut down. We are under directives to stay home, to shelter in place. Many businesses have been forced to close their doors because they are considered "non-essential." The rippling effect has placed thousands of persons on furlough or unemployment. Students are unsure of how this school year is going to end. When you do go out, you do not know if the person near you who is not complying with the 6 ft. distance directive is a carrier of the virus, even though you are masked and gloved. People are frightened and concerned about loved ones whom they cannot go see, especially their seniors. We are nervous and unsure of what is going to happen next. Yet for those who confess Jesus Christ as their Lord and Savior, there is great and enormous hope!

Over 2,033 years ago, God the Father, the Creator sent His one and only begotten Son, who took on the form of man. John 3:16 KJV reads *"For God so loved the world, that He gave His only begotten Son, that whosoever believeth in Him should not perish, but have everlasting life."* Christ came to shoulder the sins of all humankind on the cruel cross of Calvary, on that old rugged cross. The life, death, and resurrection of Jesus Christ overrides and exceeds life's circumstances, including my brothers and sisters, COVID-19. The Resurrection lies at the center, at the heart of everything we believe as disciples of Jesus Christ. If we do not believe in the Resurrection, then we might as well close the church doors, and convert the building into a CC's or Starbucks Coffee House.

During His earthly ministry, Jesus walked the roads of Galilee teaching a message of love, forgiveness, repentance and performed many miracles. People pressed through the crowds, just to touch the hem of His garment. They gathered in small and large groups to hear His words, and with open arms, Jesus received everyone-young children, tax collectors, the infirmed, the curious, and the criminal.

As Jesus shared with the disciples what was going to happen to Him, they were fearful and confused. They still, even at this point, did not fully understand Jesus' reason and purpose for being. Was dying a gruesome and humiliating death, the type of death reserved for hardened criminals, really the reason He came to earth? What about him being a royal king who would overthrow the Roman government? The future looked bleak and frightening for the disciples. This might be one of the reasons Judas betrayed Jesus.

Today, many of us are experiencing our own fears and concerns. We are facing a pandemic like nothing this generation has ever seen. While some of the latest news reports are revealing a potential glimmer of hope such as a possible drug that can work against the virus, or a possible vaccine that can inoculate us against the virus, which I read was 12 -18 months away, there are still many questions about this disease that remain unanswered. When will a sense of normalcy return to our lives? Or to put it another way, what will our new normal be? At this point, those in Washington, DC, especially "45" are playing the blame game! No need for that now. That can be done after this virus has cleared.

On Golgotha Hill, while Jesus' mother Mary, Mary Magdalene, John, and the disciples (who watched from afar) witnessed His brutal suffering on the cross, it can only be imagined that they also experienced swellings of fear and uncertainty. Yet beyond the darkness that covered their skies, God was carrying out His plan of redemption. And three days later, light overcame darkness, and hope conquered fear as Jesus rose from the dead!

Matthew, as well as the other gospel writers, lets us know, that early on Sunday morning, the women went to the tomb and found it empty. Just as

Jesus told them, on the third day, He would arise from the grave. The risen Savior appeared to the disciples and other believers several times, including to the believers walking on the road to Emmaus, and the 11 disciples who had gathered in Jerusalem. Luke tells us (Luke 24:36-39 NIV) *36 While they were still talking about this, Jesus himself stood among them and said to them, "Peace be with you."37 They were startled and frightened, thinking they saw a ghost. 38 He said to them, "Why are you troubled, and why do doubts rise in your minds? 39 Look at my hands and my feet. It is I myself! Touch me and see; a ghost does not have flesh and bones, as you see I have."* It was at this point they understood who Jesus was!

Fast forward to today. God is still on His throne weaving His cords of redemption through our lives. He loves you and me and has a plan for all of us. This, my brothers and sisters, is the glory of the Resurrection—the same hands that were pierced for our transgressions now reach out to us in compassion and forgiveness. God sent His Son to become one of us, to do for us what we could not do for ourselves. And that my brothers and sisters, is to save ourselves from the power, penalty, and punishment of sin. Truly, we can say with the prophet Isaiah, (Isaiah 53:5 KJV)" *But he was wounded for our transgressions, he was bruised for our iniquities: the chastisement of our peace was upon him; and with his stripes we are healed."*

To those of you who are overwhelmed by the cares of life right now and are burdened by the weight of the uncertainty during this season, I urge you to look to the risen Christ. He is our eternal hope!

Why? Because as the hymn writer Bill Gaither put it:

> *God sent His Son, they called Him Jesus;*
> *He came to love, heal, and forgive;*
> *He lived and died, to buy my pardon,*
> *An empty grave is there to prove my Savior lives.*
>
> *Because He lives, I can face tomorrow,*
> *Because He loves, all fear is gone.*
> *Because I know He holds the future,*
> *And life is worth the living, just because He lives.*

The way we observe this day will be vastly different from the way we have observed it in the past. It will not be about the Easter Bunny, the Easter egg hunts, new clothes, the Easter parades, the big family gatherings, the Sunday brunches. It will not even be about the young people giving Easter speeches at church. I believe, this year, in God's divine providence, the focus will be on the true meaning of this day, which is celebrating the Resurrection of our Lord and Savior Jesus Christ. It is about accepting and reaffirming Jesus as the center of your life, as your Lord and Savior.

"In times like these, we need as Savior, in times like these we need an anchor" are words to a hymn written by Ruth Caye. That anchor my brothers and sisters, is your relationship with Jesus Christ. Perhaps, there is someone today on the call who has that desire to have a closer walk, a closer relationship with Christ, to accept Jesus Christ as your Lord, meaning you will give Christ, through the power of the Holy Spirit control of your life, and Savior, meaning you know Christ died for you, and can and will save you and forgive you of your sins. There may be those who wish to reaffirm their relationship with Christ. If so, I ask that you pray these words after me, and in faith, receive them into your heart, mind, and spirit:

> Dear God*, I confess that I am a sinner*
> I have done things that are not pleasing to you*
> Lord, I am sorry*, and ask that you forgive me*
> I believe that your Son Jesus* was born of a virgin,
>   lived and died*
> That he shed his precious blood, * and died on the cross for my sin*
> I am willing to repent*, that is turn from sin* and turn my life over
>   to you. Amen

If you prayed that prayer and accepted Christ into your heart, I ask that you please share this good news with me. This is the hope and glory of the resurrection!

Let us pray: Dear Lord, I thank you for your Son Jesus Christ who was victorious over the grave. Because He lives, I have the forgiving assurance that I can face the circumstances of my life. Thank you for the guidance of the promised Comforter, the Holy Spirit. In the name of the Father, and the Son, and the Holy Spirit, Amen.

MOTHER'S DAY

Let Us Do Likewise

John 19:25-27

GREETINGS: I give a special shout out to all the mothers on the line or on ZOOM-the mothers, grandmothers and "glammas", the big mamas and Madeas, the aunties, big sisters, big cousins, the neighborhood moms, the godmothers, the play moms, the mothers who are far away, the women who have not physically birthed a child but have been there for children, mothers who are incarcerated, mothers who for whatever reason are unable to be with their children, mothers whose children are deceased, to the fathers who have assumed the role of mother, and to those mothers who are looking down from heaven. I greet you all in a very special way. It is because of the love and nurturing shown to those in your care that we are here today.

From the scripture that was read, we find ourselves at the foot of the cross with Mary the mother of Jesus, Jesus' aunt believed to be Salome, Mary the wife of Clopas, Mary Magdalene, and the beloved disciple John. Jesus is there, hanging on the cross, full of pain and agony, bearing the weight of the sins of the whole world, your sins, and my sins.

We know that Jesus was both divine and human. The divinity part of him was dealing with the eternal matters of sin. But the human side of him uttered to his mother and his beloved disciple John (John 19:26-27 NIV) 'Dear woman, here is your son,' and to the disciple, 'Here is your mother.' From that time on, this disciple took her into his home."

Following the example of Christ, I would like to share a few thoughts on how we can show our mothers love. I include not only biological mothers, but all those women who have loved and nurtured a child in any way, form, or fashion. I know for many of us, our mothers are peacefully resting with the Lord above. But these thoughts can still be shared with others, with your children and grandchildren, and other family members. I pray these words will give you enough to make a difference in the lives of women who nurture others with motherly compassion.

First of all, love her verbally. Colossians 4:6 NIV tells us *"Let your conversation be always full of grace, seasoned with salt, so that you may know how to answer everyone"* [especially mothers]. Tell her that you love her. She needs to hear that. Men, tell your wives and significant others, your daughters, your nieces, that you love them. Children, young and mature, tell the one who has loved and nurtured you that you love them. I know we put our words into action, showing them our love in tangible ways, but we still need to hear "I love you!" That is the way we as women are wired! We desire that verbal confirmation.

And then, love her physically. There was nothing as comforting as receiving that big bear hug from Big Mama. But right now, with COVID-19, we have been unable to give that hug the way we use to or plant that kiss on the cheek. We are in a time of social distancing. But, when this is all over, hugging is something we should no longer take for granted. Give your mother, your grandmother, your auntie, your children, those hugs we have been missing for the past two months. I'm sure that those who work in geriatric residential health care centers can attest to the fact that nursing home residents long for that hug, that special touch. You can tell, many are starved for that simple, innocent type of physical love. Send them virtual hugs, cards with hugs on them. Those hugs will be felt in their hearts.

Next, love her patiently. There are a lot of mothers who work outside of the home. That means, when she comes home from work, she still has the job of being Mom. Most likely she must prepare dinner, help with homework, clean the house, plus she might have some work of her own to do. During COVID-19, many moms, and grandmothers, and aunties have accepted the challenge of becoming teachers. Do not lose patience with them. The type of math and reading comprehension lessons are different from what it was when we were in school! The results remain the same. 1+9 still equals 10.

Now many of our mothers, grandmothers, great grandmothers, great aunts, and just older women who have touched our lives, have been blessed with longevity. Part of that may include slowing down physically and, in her hearing and thought processes-although some of their minds are still as sharp as a pin! Be patient. Give her a chance to say what she has to say, a chance to get to where she is going. Just remember, she was with you when you were learning how to walk, how to talk, how to put your clothes on, how to tie your shoe, how to feed yourself and deal with the mess you made. She was patient with you. Now it is our turn to show patience.

We must love mothers gratefully. The story is told of an elementary science class that was studying magnets. On the exam, the teacher had: six letters, starts with M, picks up things. What am I? What do you think over half of the class wrote-MOTHER!

Mothers and mother figures need a sincere thank you, not just today, but often, from a truly sincere heart when it's least expected. I admit that I am taking 1st Thess. 3:9 NIV out of context, but it says what needs to be expressed "...How can we thank God enough for you in return for the joy we have in the presence of our God because of you?" Actually, it may not be out of context because it is about others being brought to Christ. Most of us are here today in the presence of the Lord because of the faithfulness and prayers of those women who have nurtured us spiritually.

Finally, we are to love her honorably. Exodus 20:12 NIV reads "Honor your father and your mother, that your days may be long upon the land which the Lord your God is giving you." This is the first commandment with promise. Besides speaking politely to them and of them, it means acting in a way that shows courtesy and respect, for as long as they live. Mothers and widows have a special place in God's sight. 1st Timothy 5:3-4 NIV lets us know that we are to 3"Give proper recognition to those widows who are really in need. 4 But if a widow has children and grandchildren, these should, first of all, put their religion into practice by caring for their own family and so repaying their parents and grandparents, for this is pleasing to God." As our mothers, and fathers age, we are commanded by God to care for them. That does not mean, however, to allow yourself to become unfairly used by them. Those who find it difficult to get along with their parents, their mothers, are still commanded to honor them. Understand, we cannot willfully wrong our mothers, or fathers, and be right with God.

My brothers and sisters, as we celebrate this day as a tribute to our mothers, to those who are still with us and those who have earned their wings, and to those women in our lives who have loved us, nurtured us, disciplined us, taught us, and who have been there for us, let us remember how Jesus, despite his own anguish, made sure his mother was taken care of. Let mothers know that we love them, are patient with them, are grateful for the things they have done in our lives, and give them the honor they deserve. This is what Christ did for his mother. Let us do likewise.

Let us pray: Lord God, I thank you for the woman/women you placed in my life to nurture me in life and in my relationship with you. In Jesus name I pray, Amen

INDEPENDENCE SUNDAY
Freedom In Christ

Romans 6:1-2, Romans 7:14-25

As African-Americans, when we hear the words slave or servant, our minds almost automatically go back to thoughts of our sun-kissed ancestors who were kidnapped from the Motherland, shipped to this hemisphere as human cargo, and sold into the cruel institution of chattel slavery.

We might also think back to the days when the only jobs our parents, grandparents, and great-grandparents could get were picking produce in the fields of wealthy landowners, or as servants, cooks, chauffeurs, and nannies for affluent white families. Because of our history, it is only natural that the idea of being a servant or slave does not sit well with most of us. And with the social climate of blatant racism, the elimination of confederate statues and the demand for reparations, and Black Lives Matter being so prevalent, slavery and the atrocities of the aftermath are still systemically present in our country. To make matters worse, we have a heartless person in the White House who is truly out of touch with the realities of Covid-19.

However, as we continue to enjoy this Independence Day weekend, I want you to think of slavery and freedom from slavery from a different perspective. I want you to think of freedom from slavery from a biblical perspective. I am talking about freedom from the slavery of sin. I am talking about FREEDOM IN CHRIST!

Let us look at both Romans 6:1-2, and Romans 7:14-25. Chapter 6 begins with Paul asking the members of the Roman church, (6:1-2

NIV)*¹"What shall we say then? Shall we go on sinning that grace may increase? ²By no means! We died to sin; how can we live in it any longer?"* Some may think that if God is such a forgiving God, why not give God more to forgive. If we are guaranteed forgiveness, does that mean we have the freedom to keep on sinning?

This is akin to when I was a teen with a curfew. There were a few times that I realized I was already late and knew I was going to be in trouble. Depending on how much fun I was having, my attitude was "Well I might as well enjoy myself because I know it was going to be a long time before I'm able to get back out!" This is the same attitude some of us have toward sin. "I know God is going to forgive me, so I might as well do what I want to do." Again, Paul's answer to (vs. 1b NIV)*"Shall we go on sinning that grace may increase?"* is an emphatic no! By no means!

As it was with the Romans, many of us struggle with the magnetism of sin. Paul writes in Romans 7:15 NIV, *"I do not understand what I do. For what I want to do, I do not do, but what I hate I do."* He goes on to say in the second half of vs. 18, *"...for I have a desire to do what is good, but I cannot carry it out."*

One of the things I like about this chapter is that Paul is being very transparent. He is letting the people know that just like them, he is struggling with a sinful nature, which innately comes from Adam. Paul is filled with the Spirit of the Lord. He is planting churches and leading others to Christ with his powerful and spirit-filled preaching and teaching. However, he acknowledges that his sinful nature is still a part of him. At a point of desperation, Paul cries out, (vs. 24) *"Oh wretched man that I am! Who will rescue me from this body of death?"* Notice that Paul did not say "what will rescue me", but "who will rescue me." Paul knows whom to turn to. Vs. 25 (NIV) reads, *"Thanks be to God-through Jesus Christ our Lord."*

When we are struggling with the pull and power of sin, that tug can be powerful. When we come face to face with those temptations that can yank us away from and cause us to be out of fellowship with God, know that we can be freed from that sin through faith in our Lord and Savior Jesus Christ. Know my brothers and sisters, that freedom from sin is possible because of what Jesus did for you and me on Calvary. He died on that old, rugged cross to forgive our sins, so that we would not have to carry the guilt and shame of our iniquities.

But like Paul, we must first acknowledge our sins. John, the son of Zebedee wrote (1st John 1:8 NIV), *"If we claim to be without sin, we deceive ourselves, and the truth is not in us."* Or as I've heard it said, "Ya lyin' and the truth ain't in ya!" (vs.9) *If we confess our sins, he is faithful and just, and will forgive us our sins and purify us from all unrighteousness."* John continues by saying (2:1) *"My dear children, I write to you so you will not sin. But, if anyone does sin, we have one who speaks to the Father in our defense-Jesus Christ, the righteous one!"* Jesus conquered sin once and for all, and promises that if we look to Him, we will not have to continually give in to the temptations of sin. We can, my brothers and sisters, have freedom from the slavery of sin. We can have FREEDOM IN CHRIST!

Now! Do not get it twisted! Emancipation from sin does not come automatically. Some people think that when they become a Christian, their lives will be silky smooth with no more struggles, no more temptations, no financial problems, no family conflicts. Understand that the old sinful nature is still there, trying to get the upper hand. A lot of Christians, both new and seasoned, you and I, have experienced that conflict to the point of saying, "I might as well give up!" It is at this point that we are likely to fall back under the slavery of sin. We blow it and fail to have victory over sin.

Being born again, that is accepting Jesus Christ as your Lord and Savior takes a moment of faith, a leap of faith if you will. It is a starting point. But becoming Christ-like is a life-long ongoing process. As we grow on our Christian journey, that old sinful nature becomes increasingly subdued, restrained. We are never released from the necessity of choosing to go God's way, that is being led by the Holy Spirit. We will still have our temptations and moments of weakness. However, the key is to allow the Spirit of Jesus Christ to have dominance and authority in your life. That my brothers and sisters comes through prayer, in season and out of season. It comes by studying, meditating, reflecting on, and applying the Word of God to our lives. And it comes by being in fellowship with those who are also striving to grow in Christ. Roman 6:22 NIV says *"But now that you have been set free from sin and become slaves to God, the benefit you reap leads to holiness, and the result is eternal life."*

My brothers and sisters, know that freedom from sin is possible because Christ died for our sins, rose from the dead, and ascended into heaven to be the Advocate for our forgiveness. Know that freedom from sin does not just happen automatically, because we still have a natural Adamic sinful nature. But thanks be to God, the good news is, when we yield to the Spirit of the Lord and live our lives under the guidance of the Holy Spirit, we gain freedom from sin. When we make daily decisions to go God's way, we will see that old sinful nature coming under the control of Jesus Christ, and we become stronger and stronger, enabling us to defeat sin. There truly is my brothers and sisters, FREEDOM IN CHRIST!

Let us pray: Lord God, help me to be guided by Your Holy Spirit to overcome sin and to live my life in such a way that I can truly have freedom in Christ. In the matchless name of Jesus I pray, Amen.

PRESIDENTAL ELECTION

The Stewardship
Of Citizenship

Matthew 22:15-21

This time last year, as we were preparing to go to the polls to elect our governor, and others, I preached a sermon entitled "The Stewardship of Citizenship. I emphasized that beyond the stewardship of our time, talents, and treasures, we also have the responsibility of being good stewards of our citizenship. I stated that we are first responsible to God. It was Jesus who told the Pharisees, (Matthew 22:21 KJV) *"Render therefore to Caesar the things that are Caesar's, and to God the things that are God's."* The things that are of God include worship, prayer, studying God's Word, loving others, forgiving others, doing those things which are pleasing in the sight of God. We also have a responsibility to our governments at all levels, and to ourselves to be good citizens. That means, among other things, exercising our right and privilege to vote. We are now 3 days away from an election of great historic significance.

As a people, as African-Americans, for us not to vote is to dishonor those who came before us, those who suffered the brutality of white supremacy for the right to vote, those who gave their lives so that future generations, you and I would be able to freely exercise our right to vote.

With that being said, I believe most of you have already voted, either by early voting or absentee ballot. As a quick reminder, absentee ballots must be in the registrar's office by tomorrow, November 2nd. For those who have not yet voted, as I stated in the newsletter, be prepared for a long wait. Double-check your polling location before you go. Make sure you have the proper ID you need. Take a chair and something cold to drink. And do not be intimidated by anyone who might try to discourage you from voting. GEAUX VOTE!

When we think of stewardship, what usually comes to mind is the stewardship of our treasure, our money, that is what we give to the Lord in tithes and offerings. This is, however, an extremely limited and inadequate definition of stewardship. Yes, we are to be faithful and good stewards of the treasures God has blessed us to receive. We are responsible to God for how we earn, spend, save, invest, and give of our finances. We are also stewards of our time, which is a precious commodity. We can waste and misuse time, or we can use it for the glory of God, for the good of others, and our own happiness. We are also stewards of the gifts and talents that God has given every one of us. We are responsible to God and to our brothers and sisters for how we use our talents. Additionally, as Christians, we are stewards of our testimony, meaning, how we share with others the good news of serving a true and living God, and how God has worked in our lives.

Again, I want to share with you "THE STEWARDSHIP OF CITIZENSHIP-THE PRESIDENTIAL ELECTION EDITION. My brothers and sisters, we know what is at stake with the presidential, senatorial, and congressional elections, as well as with local elections. My purpose this morning is to help us to understand our role as Christians in the realm of politics. Some Christians believe church and politics should not mix. I, however, totally disagree. We <u>must</u> be involved so that we can impact and influence the political realm with positive Christian values.

First, as Christians, we do have responsibilities toward our government. In Matthew 22:15-22, Jesus is teaching, not preaching, but teaching about that responsibility. As usual, the Pharisees were trying to corner Jesus with a trick question. In this particular instance, the Pharisees were joined by the Herodians, Jews who were loyal to the Roman government. Normally the two sects were at odds with one another but in this case, they came together against their common "headache" Jesus. They are trying to flatter Jesus by telling him that they knew he had integrity, how he accurately taught God's truths, how he was not swayed by the opinions of others, and that he didn't misuse those who followed him. They then asked the question, (vs. 17b NIV) *"Is it right to pay taxes to Caesar or not?* Looking at vss. 18-21 (MSG), it reads *[18-19] Jesus knew they were up to no good. He said, "Why are you playing these games with me? Why are you trying to trap me? Do you have a coin? Let me see it." They handed him a silver piece. [20] "This engraving—who does it look like? And whose name is on it?" [21] They said, "Caesar." "Then give Caesar what is his, and give God what is his."* The NKJV says *[21] "And He said to them, "Render therefore to Caesar the things that are Caesar's, and to God the things that are God's."*

Jesus avoided their trap by showing them, and us, that we have dual citizenship. Our citizenship in the country, state, parish, and municipalities require that we pay taxes for the services and benefits we receive, as well as being a part of the governmental process, namely, VOTING! However, our citizenship in the Kingdom of God requires that we pledge our primary obedience and commitment to God.

I ask the question, how do we put the Stewardship of Citizenship into practice? How do we render to Caesar the things that are Caesar's, and to God the things that are God's? The first thing we must do is pray. Pray for our nation, our state, our parish, and our municipalities. Pray that those in leadership, in power will humble themselves before the Lord. We must pray that those who are elected will truly have the heart and well-being of the people they represent at the forefront of the decisions they make. In this critical time in the life of our country, we have to pray that those making the decisions on how to deal with and eradicate this coronavirus will be led by God, as well as science. We know that this virus has led to an unprecedented increase in economic hardship for families and businesses, an uprise in emotional and mental stress, anger issues, domestic violence and child abuse, families fighting against one another.

2nd Chronicles 7:14 NIV tells us *[14] If My people who are called by My name will humble themselves, and pray and seek My face, and turn from their wicked ways, then I will hear from heaven, and will forgive their sin and heal their land."* It has got to start at the top. That is why we must pray for our leaders, from the White House, whoever will occupy it for the next four years, to the state capital, to our house, and at every level in between.

And then, we too have to pray for ourselves, individually and collectively. We must pray for the guidance of the Holy Spirit to "do the right thing." We must confess our sins to the Lord and trust in the Lord's forgiveness. There are generational sins that have plagued families, past and present such as domestic violence, infidelity, drug and alcohol addictions, emotional abandonment. These spill over into and affect our communities. Ask God to forgive those sins and to bring healing to hurting hearts and spirits. Also, pray that God will use you to show and help others experience the unconditional love of Jesus Christ, especially those who do not know Him.

Next, we must put people before politics. Jesus always put people first. Most of the conflicts and challenges Jesus had with the Pharisees were because he put the needs of the people before the religious laws. For example, Matthew 12:11-14, lets us know he healed a man's hand on the Sabbath. The Jewish leaders asked him if it was lawful to heal on the Sabbath. Healing was considered work, and it was unlawful to work on the Sabbath. After giving an example of a sheep falling into a pit, Jesus asked (vs. 11b NIV) *"…will you not take hold of it and lift it out".* Of course, they looked dumbfounded. He ended this challenge by saying (vs. 12 NIV) *"Therefore, it is lawful to do good on the Sabbath."*

Luke 13:10-17 tells us that while teaching in the synagogue on the Sabbath, Jesus called forward a woman who had an infirmity that caused her to be bent over for eighteen years. Jesus healed her. Not only was the issue that this happened on the Sabbath, but it was also the fact that she was a woman. As a church body, we too, especially during this epidemic, must put the needs of the people before the laws of the church.

Unfortunately, we have a person in the White House who has consistently put his agenda, his wants, his ego, ahead of the people. This is evident by the fact that even as the virus continued and continues to surge, which he still downplays, he is holding rallies, full of persons not social distancing, not telling the people to "mask up," creating what the scientist call "super spreader" events. But you know what, I do not put all of the blame on 45. God gives us free will, and those who attend these events choose to place themselves in those environments. Many of them did become ill with Covid-19. Yes, we know that God is in charge, but I believe that God allows people and situations to be in places that harm society and us personally because we are not doing what we should be doing.

Next, the Stewardship of Citizenship involves being engaged. By this, I mean that our task as God's people is to make the influence of Jesus Christ felt in all areas of our lives-home, school, job, online, wherever we are. Does this mean we are to be Bible thumpin', big cross wearing, scripture quotin', "hallelujah, praise the Lord" type people? No, it does not. It means that we are to carry ourselves in such a way that others see the grace of God, the love of Jesus Christ, and the guidance of the Holy Spirit in our walk, in our talk, and in the way we deal with others. It means we engage in respectable conversation; we listen to those whose opinions are different from ours and work together to find solutions and common ground.

Being engaged also means being informed about the issues and the candidates. Avail yourselves to news from a variety of sources from across the political spectrum. That means listening to both Joe Biden and Donald Trump, Kamala Harris and John Pence, Adrian Perkins and Bill Cassidy. I found that watching the presidential and vice-presidential debates to be most enlightening. They confirmed something I already knew- and that is whom I was voting for as president. One Christian writer said, "Our knowledge of a subject/candidate is limited by the resources we consult." Get the full spectrum, both positive and negative by watching CNN, BET, PBS, Fox, NBC, ABC, and CBS news. If you are a late-night TV watcher, check out Don Lemon, Andrew Cuomo, and others, including Fox's Hannity.

As Christians, we need to know where candidates stand morally and spiritually. Do their lives represent Godly principles? Have they sought guidance through prayer? Who are the candidates who will put people first, ahead of political party affiliations, business ventures, and personal opportunities? Look at the track records of the candidates. What have they done in the past? What are their plans for the future? Choose wisely! The STEWARDSHIP OF CITIZENSHIP means being engaged and informed.

Finally, the STEWARDSHIP OF CITIZENSHIP reaches its peak Tuesday, November 3rd. Our vote is our voice. Understand that the politics of America, Louisiana, Tangipahoa Parish, and local municipalities are not the voice of everyone, but just the voice of those who vote. Let me repeat that! .... The politics of America, Louisiana, Tangipahoa Parish, and local municipalities are not the voice of everyone, but just the voice of those who vote. If you don't vote, you don't have a voice. Know, that your vote matters. Choose wisely.

In addressing the Congressional Black Caucus Foundation before the 2016 presidential election, former President Barack Obama said, *"There's no such thing as a vote that doesn't matter. It all matters. And after we achieved historic turnout in 2008 and 2012, especially in the African-American community, I will consider it a personal insult, an insult to my legacy, if this community lets down its guard and fails to activate itself in this election. You want to give me a good sendoff?* GO VOTE!"

To the young adults, the Millennials, your vote matters. To the seniors, the Baby Boomers, and beyond, your vote matters. To the 18-year-olds eligible to vote for the first time, your vote matters. And then, do not go to the polls alone. Take your spouse, your significant other, your "boo", your young adults, your nieces, your nephews, grandparents, neighbors. Make your voice heard.

Know my brothers and sisters, that just like we have a God-ordained stewardship responsibility for the use of our time, talent, and treasure, we have a God-ordained responsibility to practice the STEWARDSHIP OF CITIZENSHIP. Remember the words of our Lord and Savior Jesus Christ-." And He said to them, (Matthew 22:21 NIV) *"Render therefore to Caesar the things that are Caesar's, and to God the things that are God's."*

Let us pray: Dear Lord, please guide me in being a good responsible citizen of both Your Kingdom and my community. In Jesus name I pray, Amen.

THANKSGIVING

Don't Skip Over Thanksgiving

1st Chronicles 16:7-12, 34-36

This scripture tells of David giving thanks to the Lord for being able to bring the Ark of the Covenant to Jerusalem. The Ark of the Covenant was the most sacred object of the Hebrew faith. It was a large gold-covered wooden box that contained the stone tablets on which the Ten Commandments were written, a pot of manna, and Aaron's rod which grew blossoms. David had already made Jerusalem the nation's political center, and by bringing the Ark of the Covenant to Jerusalem, he was now making that city the nation's center for worship. There was a great celebration of thanksgiving with music, singing, and dancing, all in praise to God Almighty. One of my favorite movies is Raiders of the Lost Ark. The movie centers around the Ark, which archeologist Indiana Jones and others believed had supernatural powers. It was believed by the Nazis, that whoever possessed the Ark would rule the world. That's Hollywood!

A couple of weeks ago, I went to my favorite dollar store to find some inexpensive Thanksgiving decorations. I shared with you earlier that my siblings and I had a virtual pre-thanksgiving dinner and I wanted to have some type of Thanksgiving-themed decorations on the table. When I walked into the store, I was bombarded with three aisles of Christmas decorations, everything from lights, to stockings, to gingerbread house kits, to wreaths, to Santa Claus figurines. You name it, they had it. I looked high and low for anything with a Thanksgiving theme. Finally, toward the middle of the store in the back, I saw just a few Thanksgiving items, such as paper plates and napkins, and a few ceramic mugs, nothing that I wanted or could use.

As I was leaving that store, I began to think, what happened to Thanksgiving? Has it been forgotten? Does our society not think that it's important to give thanks? It used to be that Thanksgiving kicked off the Christmas season, but now it seems like it is Halloween that gets the Christmas season started. There are even stores that have had Christmas decorations out since the beginning of October.

The media has been airing the Christmas commercials for at least two weeks-the Hershey's Kisses, the GEICO commercial where the man is decorating his house that can be seen from outer space, the Coca-Cola commercial with the polar bears, the Toyota commercial where the husband has purchased trucks for his wife and himself. By the time Thanksgiving gets here, we will already be so overwhelmed with Christmas, that our holiday stress level will have already risen. That stress can also be about the shopping and holiday finances or thinking about household projects you want to complete before the relatives come to visit, which will be very different this year. The sad part is, nothing I've seen or heard so far has had anything to do with the birth of Christ.

This year the usual holiday stress factors will be unlike anything we've experienced in the past. We are dealing with Covid-19, which has placed unprecedented challenges on all of us. For many, it has to do with finances. "I've been out of work and I won't be able to do what I usually do for the holidays." Family gatherings will be different. I read in yesterday's Baton Rouge Advocate an article about an interview with Dr. Anthony Fauci. He said that "families should consider factors such as age, underlying conditions, travel, testing and quarantining of people who wish to dine together on the holiday." That means you may need to reconsider going to grandma's who is in that high-risk category, especially if there are other underlying conditions, and if you have been "out and about." He went on to say "I'm saying everyone needs to seriously think about the risk-benefit ratio. In other words, is the benefit I will get from going to someone else's house worth the risk of getting sick or making someone else sick."

There will be less traveling to spend Thanksgiving or Christmas with relatives in other cities. One of my favorite Christmas songs is "It's the Most Wonderful Time of the Year." For many, many families, this will not be the most wonderful time of the year because they will experience for the first time, a holiday season without a loved one who succumbed to the virus or other illness.

I raise the question, why have we, as a society, skipped over the true essence and meaning of Thanksgiving. We know that Thanksgiving is supposed to be a day when we as a nation take the time to intentionally give thanks to God for God's many blessings. For so many, Thanksgiving is just an American holiday on the calendar in which we get an extra-long weekend. For those in Louisiana, in the past, it was the day to prepare to go to the Bayou Classic. This last Thursday in November is the day many get up early to watch the New York Macy's or the Detroit Thanksgiving Parades and welcome Santa Claus to town. Before the virus, this was the day for families to come together, ridiculously stuff themselves, watch football, and then camp out overnight at the malls for the Black Friday sales. However, these are not the true meanings of Thanksgiving.

I'd like to offer three reasons why we should not skip over Thanksgiving. First of all, thanksgiving, being grateful, showing God gratitude should be a way of life, and not just a one-day thing! Praise and thanksgiving should be a regular part of our daily lives, and not reserved for celebrations. Every morning when we open our eyes, every morning the Lord wakes us up is a day of thanksgiving. When you arise in the morning, you and I need to thank God for the night's rest and for God having us on God's wake-up list. Thank God throughout the day for meeting your needs, for providing food, clothing, and shelter. Thank God for your family. Thank God that you have not contracted the virus. And if you did get sick, thank God that God allowed you to overcome the illness.

Thank God for everything. 1ˢᵗ Thess. 5:16-18 NIV tells us to *"¹⁶Be joyful always, ¹⁷ pray continually, ¹⁸ give thanks in ALL circumstances, for this is God's will for you in Christ Jesus."* And then at the close of the day, thank God for the day's journey, for protecting you from dangers seen and unseen. Ask God to forgive you for anything you might have done which was not pleasing in God's eyesight. And then ask God to give you a peaceful night's rest, to wake you in the morning, being thankful for another chance to give God the praise and another chance to "get it right."

Next, true thankfulness, true gratitude is a mark of God's community. We, as a Body of Believers, should be thankful that, despite our church building being closed, we are still able to come together to worship, to pray together, to study God's Word together, to have love and compassion for one another. We should thank God for every one of us. We are a church family, and like most families, we will have our ups and downs. But after all has been said and done, we are to be thankful to God that we have each other as a church family.

And then, recognize the benefits of a thankful heart. As we give thanks to God, we become less selfish and are more confident in who God is. When we express gratitude to God, it refocuses our attention from ourselves and all that is going on around us. At this time in our lives, there are so many distractions-the White House transition, COVID-19, the economy, family issues. Sometimes my brothers and sisters, because of all the vicissitudes of life that come our way, it is hard to realize the many blessings God has bestowed upon us. When we shift our focus to remembering what God has done for us, it is hard not to be thankful.

When we think of the benefits of being thankful, know that gratitude refreshes our faith. Being thankful keeps us from allowing ourselves to have pity parties when we are discouraged, or when we are facing life's challenges. Having that faithful gratitude lets you know that you can (Hebrew 11:1 NIV) *"...be sure of what you hope for and certain of what you do not see."*. Being thankful strengthens our faith, our spirituality, and our walk with God. When we continuously praise God, we will find that we don't and won't take the blessings of God for granted.

Going back to when I was trying to find some thanksgiving decorations for my table, I did leave the store upset and had to go look elsewhere, wondering why we as a society seem to skip over Thanksgiving. Now, I understand all of the economic issues businesses are faced with trying to boost sales and have some type of profit margin, especially in this season of the pandemic. However, for us as believers, this is not a problem. It does not matter that the nation skips over the true meaning and essence of Thanksgiving. As believers, it does not matter that we may not be able to have the big Thanksgiving family dinner, go shopping for the Black Friday sales, or go to the Bayou Classic. We do not have to wait until November 26th to give thanks. Why? Because we know that EVERY DAY IS A DAY OF THANKSGIVING. The songwriter Leonard Burks put it this way:

Every day is a day of thanksgiving.
God's been so good to me,
Every day He's blessing me.
Every day is a day of thanksgiving;
Take the time to glorify the Lord today.
He keeps blessing me, (over and over) blessing me;
He opens the door, that I might see,
He's blessing me.
He keeps blessing me, blessing me...
Take the time to glorify the Lord today.

Let us pray: Lord, let me not get so caught up in anticipating the secular, materialistic celebration of Christmas, that I don't take the time to be thankful for your many blessings. In Jesus name I pray, Amen.

ADVENT

Who Is Jesus The Christ?

John 1:1-5, 14

Even during this pandemic, people are out and about, shopping, eating, attending trees lighting festivals, and just enjoying the holiday season. Many are masked, observing the protocols that have been put in place by the CDC and the governor. However, some are completely ignoring those safety precautions. If you are "out and about," please make sure you keep yourself and your loved ones safe.

We have become such a secular society, that I cannot help but wonder, do people really know who or what they are celebrating. Do children, who are being bombarded with toy and game commercials know the true significance of giving their parents, grandparents, aunties, and uncles that long list of items they want for Christmas? Do they really know and understand the "reason for the season?"

As members of the Body of Christ, most of us know. But just in case we need help in telling others, in sharing the Good News with those who do not know or are not sure, this morning, I want to answer the question, WHO IS JESUS CHRIST?

First of all, Jesus Christ is the fulfillment of Isaiah's prophecy found in the book of Isaiah 7:14 KJV. *"Therefore the Lord himself shall give you a sign; Behold, a virgin shall conceive, and bear a son, and shall call his name Immanuel* [meaning God with us.] The Bible lets us know that Jesus was both fully human and fully God. Although he took upon himself full humanity and lived as a man, as a human like you and me, he never ceased to be the eternal God who has always existed. He is the Creator and Sustainer of all things, the source of eternal life.

What Jesus taught and what Jesus did are tied inseparably to who he was and is. In other words, in his humanity, Jesus not only talked the talk, but he also truly walked the walk. Jesus ministered firsthand to those around him. He fed the hungry, healed the lame, gave comfort to the comfortless, lifted the fallen. He had his circle of disciples whom he taught by precept and example how to live as believers. As Christians celebrating the birth of Christ, should we do any less? We should live our lives by the examples taught and set by Jesus Christ. Let others see Christ in you!

Next, Jesus is the Light of the World. John 1:9 NIV reads, *"The true light that gives light to everyone was coming into the world."* That means that light was coming for you and me. Throughout the New Testament, the followers of Jesus are called to be lights in the darkness. That means we are to let our light shine. As believers living in a world filled with the darkness of hate, violence, and confusion, we must cast off the works of darkness (that which is not of Christ) by putting on the light of Christ. Matthew tells us in 5:16 NIV, *"…let your light shine before men, that they may see your good deeds and praise your Father in heaven."*

We must live our lives in such a way that others see the light and love of Christ within us. Would your family, neighbors, your co-workers, classmates, and even your church members see the same person today that they see Monday-Saturday? Are you consistent in your Christian walk? How do you respond when someone bumps you in a crowd, especially during this time of COVID-19 and social distancing, or cuts you off in traffic? What will others see in your responses? Would they see you flying off the handle and cussing, or would they see you with a calmness and "peace that passes all understanding?"

I think David has a word to help us in those challenging times. (Ps. 119:11 KJV) *"Thy word have I hid in my heart that I might not sin against thee."* Study and know God's Word so that when you are faced with challenging trials or situations, you will be able to let your light, the light of Jesus Christ shine through you. The Psalmist also wrote, (Ps. 119:105 KJV) *"Thy Word is a lamp unto my feet and a light unto my path."* Be guided by the light of God through Jesus Christ, and the empowerment of the Holy Spirit.

Finally, Jesus is the Messiah. In both Judaism and Christianity, Messiah means the promised "anointed one" or the Christ. As Christians, we believe that Jesus was and is the Messiah who came to deliver humankind, to deliver you and me from our sins. He was the fulfillment of the Old Testament prophecies that spoke of the Messiah's blessing of the Jewish nation. The Jews however did not give proper attention to the prophecies. They missed the memo that was saying Christ would bring salvation to the entire world, not just the Jews. They kind of "sluffed" over that part of the prophecy. Luke made it clear to his Greek audience, as well as the Jews, that Christ came to save all of humanity from their sins, both Jew and Gentile.

There is a clique that says, "the proof is in the pudding." Even though he did not have to, Jesus proved that he was the Messiah. He performed observable deeds and miracles, from turning water into wine to feeding the 5000 to healing individuals of their infirmities, to his resurrection and his ascension into heaven. His contemporaries saw and reported the acts of Christ for us to read today. Jesus ministered to the world with actions that one could see, feel, smell, taste, and touch. (Psalm 34:8a KJV) *"O taste and see that the Lord is good";* (Matthew 9:20 NIV) *"...touched the hem of his garment";* (John 9:25b NIV)*"...I was blind, but now I see."* Scientists call that empirical evidence. Isaiah 35:5-6 NIV reads [5]*"Then will the eyes of the blind be opened and the ears of the deaf unstopped.[6] Then will the lame leap like a deer, and the mute tongue shout for joy. Water will gush forth in the wilderness and streams in the desert."* We would be hard-pressed not to recognize Jesus Christ as the Messiah, our Lord and Savior.

Amid COVID-19, we know this Christmas will be different. Those big family gatherings, visiting one another in homes, traveling to see grandma and grandpa, whether near or far will be much less, if at all. This virus is real people, and we must be mindful of our going and coming, who we are around, especially our "seasoned" adults.

As a quick aside regarding our seniors, if you are a caregiver, especially a young one, when you are out, be sure to be extra careful in following the safety and protocols established by the CDC. You do not want to bring anything into the environment that could affect or infect the one in your care. So many seniors, who have been safely quarantined have contracted the virus from others who brought it into the house.

My beloved brothers and sisters. Know that we are not without hope. As we continue this 2020 Advent journey and we prepare to celebrate the birth of our Lord and Savior Jesus Christ, our hope is in knowing who Jesus Christ is and why he came. Just to be clear, know that Christ came to save us from our sins, to bring hope, joy, peace, and, love into this world, and to teach us how to love one another. This is how we answer the question, who is Jesus the Christ!

God has given us the greatest gift we can ever receive. If you have not accepted that gift, the gift of Jesus Christ as your Lord and Savior, then this is your opportunity to give Christ the greatest gift you can give, a gift more precious than the gifts of gold, frankincense, and myrrh given to the Christ Child at his birth by the Wise Men. Give Jesus Christ your heart, that he may, through the power of the Holy Spirit, dwell in you, so he can lead you and guide you, and direct you today, during this Advent season, and throughout your Christian journey.

Let us pray: Lord God, I thank you for the greatest gift I could ever receive, your Son Jesus the Christ. As I go about preparing to celebrate the birth of the Messiah, let me share the true meaning of Christmas. JESUS IS THE REASON FOR THE SEASON. Amen.

Epilogue

As stated in the Introduction, it is my sincere prayer that after reading and meditating on these messages, you will be able to answer the question **"WHAT WILL GET US THROUGH?"** We know that it is our faith and trust in God. Even though the messages centered around the COVID-19 virus, the answer can be applied to whatever challenging situation we may face.

This year, Louisiana, Mississippi, Texas, and Arkansas experienced unprecedented freezing that caused extensive property damage and loss of life. Additionally, torrential rain caused much flooding in areas still reeling from recent natural calamities, including hurricanes and tornados. I know those in the metropolitan Baton Rouge area were having flashbacks to the 2016 flood. We still have the 2021 hurricane season (June-November) to face. Even though property was lost, many were quick to say that it is their faith in God that got them through, and it is their faith in God that will continue to see them through these trying times.

As we prepare to go to press, much has transpired since the beginning of the pandemic. The Biden/Harris administration has settled into the nation's capital, vaccines have been developed by Pfizer, Moderno, and Johnson and Johnson to eradicate the Covid-19 virus, and the 1st anniversary of the George Floyd killing has been observed, with his family meeting with President Biden at the White House.

The nation is opening up. The mask mandate has been lifted in many states, even though nationally, as of May 25, 2021, only 39% of the adult population has been fully vaccinated.[1] President Biden had set a goal that by July 4, 2021, 70% of the nation's adults will have at least received the first shot.[2] Unfortunately, "As of July 3, around 67 percent of American adults have been vaccinated, according to the Centers for Disease Control and Prevention (CDC)."[3]

The vaccine is now available to young people ages 12-16 years of age, and as of November 2021, the Phizer vaccine can be received by children ages 5-11. Many school boards however are still debating whether students should be required to wear masks and follow other CDC protocols. Most businesses and restaurants are fully open. More and more houses of worship are having in-person worship services, still following the protocol established by the CDC. They come together as a body of believers, rejoicing that they can again worship together in the house of the Lord.

In mid-July of 2021, only 31% of the Louisiana adult population had received the vaccine. This is not good. The nation is now faced with the Delta variant that scientists say is more contagious than the original Covid-19 virus. It has been reported there is a surge in virus-related hospitalizations, and 83% of the patients are those who have not received the vaccine. With the surge of the Delta variant, we are a nation that might be forced to revert to being "shut down."

And now in December of 2021, a new coronavirus variant Omicron is emerging. Case have been reported in California, New York, and Minnesota, and seems to be rapidly spreading, including Louisiana. By the time this book reaches publication, it can very well be spread throughout the United States.

Regardless of these circumstances, praise will continue to abound among the people of God, thanking God for seeing them through these and other difficult times. My beloved brothers and sisters, again, I ask the question "What will get us through?" As we go forth, let us do so knowing and trusting that it is God, belief in God's Son Jesus the Christ, and the guidance of the Holy Spirit that will get us through.

Be Blessed! "Rev. Pat"

1   usafacts.org/visualizations/covid-vaccine-tracker-states/
2   edition.cnn.com/2021/05/04/politics/biden-covid-goals-july-4/index.html
3   theuspost.com/Health experts explain what it means to miss Biden's goal of 70% of US adults vaccinated by July 4

Printed in the United States
by Baker & Taylor Publisher Services